SHORT NATURE WALKS

ON CAPE COD, NANTUCKET, AND THE VINEYARD

Praise for previous editions:

"Any hiker or casual walker will appreciate this book . . . not only are the walks fully defined, but helpful suggestions are offered that inform those wishing to escape the humdrum of daily routine for a short time just what to look for on the walks. . . ."

—*Ellsworth* **(Maine)** *American*

"A handy little book for a restful and pleasant stay on the Cape."

—*Travel Agent Magazine*

"Whether a native or a casual vacationer, the walker will find the book to be one of essential reference, and patrons of the outdoor arts will experience a new dimension of pleasure as they stroll the paths described in this very informative and useful book."

—*The Cape Cod Times*

". . . directions, narrative, and maps for memorable strolls and hikes."

—*Northeast Outdoors*

SHORT NATURE WALKS
ON CAPE COD, NANTUCKET, AND THE VINEYARD

Seventh Edition

Hugh and Heather Sadlier

Revised by
Karl Luntta

The Globe Pequot Press

Guilford, Connecticut

Cover photo: Pat O'Hara/Stone
Cover design: Lana Mullen
Photo credits: pp. 88–89, 90, 100, and 104–5 by Karl Luntta.

Library of Congress Cataloging-in-Publication Data

Sadlier, Hugh.
   Short nature walks on Cape Cod, Nantucket, and the Vineyard / Hugh and Heather Sadlier. — 7th ed. / revised by Karl Luntta.
      p.   cm. — (Short nature walk series)
   ISBN 0-7627-0939-1
   1. Hiking—Massachusetts—Cape Cod—Guidebooks.   2. Hiking—Massachusetts—Martha's Vineyard—Guidebooks.   3. Hiking—Massachusetts—Nantucket Island—Guidebooks.   4. Nature study—Massachusetts—Cape Cod.   5. Nature study—Massachusetts—Martha's Vineyard.   6. Nature study—Massachusetts—Nantucket Island.   7. Cape Cod (Mass.)—Guidebooks.   8. Martha's Vineyard (Mass.)—Guidebooks.   9. Nantucket Island (Mass.)—Guidebooks.   I. Sadlier, Heather.   II. Luntta, Karl, 1955-.   III. Title. IV. Series.

GV199.42.M42C367   2001   2001023018
917.44'90444—dc21

Manufactured in the United States of America
Seventh Edition/First Printing

Help Us Keep This Guide Up to Date

Every effort has been made by the authors and editors to make this guide as accurate and useful as possible. However, many things can change after a guide is published—establishments close, phone numbers change, facilities come under new management, etc.

We would love to hear from you concerning your experiences with this guide and how you feel it could be made better and be kept up to date. While we may not be able to respond to all comments and suggestions, we'll take them to heart, and we'll also make certain to share them with the author. Please send your comments and suggestions to the following address:

The Globe Pequot Press
Reader Response/Editorial Department
P.O. Box 480
Guilford, CT 06437

Or you may e-mail us at:

editorial@globe-pequot.com

Thanks for your input, and happy travels!

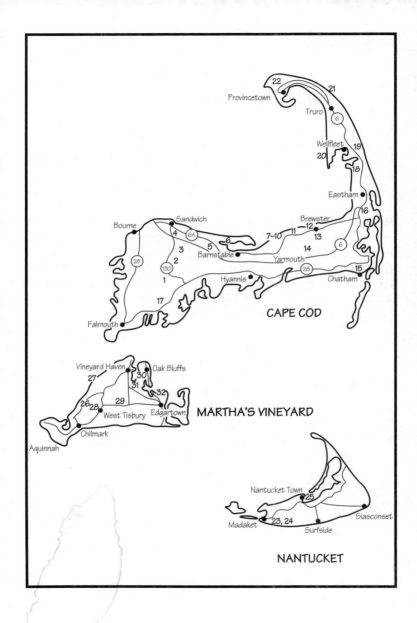

Provincetown
22
21
Truro
6
Wellfleet
19
20
18
Eastham
16
Sandwich
Brewster
Bourne
4
6A
6
7-10
11
12
13
3
5
14
Barnstable
Yarmouth
6
130
2
28
1
15
Hyannis
28
Chatham
17
CAPE COD
Falmouth

Vineyard Haven
Oak Bluffs
27
30
31
32
26
28
29
MARTHA'S VINEYARD
West Tisbury
Edgartown
Chilmark
Aquinnah

Nantucket Town
25
Siasconset
Madaket
23, 24
Surfside
NANTUCKET

Contents

Introduction ix

Cape Cod

1. Ashumet Holly and Wildlife Sanctuary 1
2. Lowell Holly Reservation 5
3. Ryder Conservation Lands 9
4. The Old Briar Patch 13
5. Talbot's Point Conservation Lands 17
6. Sandy Neck 21
7. Callery-Darling Conservation Area: Eastern Trail 25
8. Callery-Darling Conservation Area: Western Trail 29
9. Yarmouth Historical Society Nature Trails 33
10. John Wing Trail 37
11. Cape Cod Museum of Natural History: North Trail 41
12. Cape Cod Museum of Natural History: South Trail 45
13. Stoney Brook Mill Sites 49
14. Harding's Beach 53
15. Fort Hill Trail 57
16. Buttonbush Trail 61
17. Quashnet Corridor 65
18. Wellfleet Bay Wildlife Sanctuary 69
19. Atlantic White Cedar Swamp Trail 73
20. Great Island Trail 77
21. Pilgrim Spring Trail 81
22. Beech Forest Trail 85

Nantucket

23. Long Pond Trail 91
24. The Sanford Farm, Ram Pasture, and the Woods 95
25. Windswept Cranberry Bog 99

Martha's Vineyard

26. Waskosim's Rock Reservation.. 107

27. Cedar Tree Neck Sanctuary 111

28. Middle Road Sanctuary 115

29. Manuel F. Correllus State Forest 119

30. Felix Neck Wildlife Sanctuary 123

31. Caroline Tuthill Preserve and Dark Woods 127

32. Sheriff's Meadow Sanctuary 131

Introduction

Cape Cod's hiking trails lead to endless pleasures and discoveries. A sample of what awaits you includes sunsets topping shifting sand dunes; shaded walks along needle-covered paths coupled with wide-stretching vistas across sand and marsh, blossoming shadbush, beach plums, and *Rosa rugosa;* peaceful wanderings along deserted, snow-flecked trails; and—of course—wildlife: from cottontail rabbits with twitching noses and bobbing tails to the graceful soaring of majestic ospreys; from sideways scamperings of fiddler crabs to raucous callings of herring gulls.

The Thirty-two Walks

Twenty-two of the walks in this book are on Cape Cod, three are on Nantucket, and seven are on Martha's Vineyard. They explore woods, marshes, swamps, seashores, dunes, kettle holes, drumlins, ponds, streams, and wildlife sanctuaries. They take you to an island and a braille trail. All follow established trails that are either well marked or easily recognized.

Most of the walks provide opportunities to observe and appreciate nature at a leisurely pace. A few will challenge your muscles and bring sweat to your brow.

New Areas

Since the mid-1980s, a number of properties have been acquired by towns and semi-public foundations for conservation purposes. These properties are in a constant state of development as new trails are added and old ones are refurbished. For information on new trails not described in this edition, please contact the following offices and groups:

Conservation Commissions/Natural Resource Departments/Town Halls

Barnstable Natural Resources Department
    (508) 790–6272
    1189 Phinney's Lane
    Hyannis, MA 02601

Bourne Conservation Commission
    (508) 759–0625
    Town Hall
    24 Perry Avenue
    Buzzards Bay, MA 02532

Brewster Conservation Office
    (508) 896–3701
    Town Hall
    2198 Main Street
    Brewster, MA 02631

Chatham Conservation Foundation
    (508) 945–4084
    Town Hall
    549 Main Street
    Chatham, MA 02633

Dennis Conservation Commission
    (508) 394–8300
    Town Hall
    485 Main Street, P.O. Box 1419
    South Dennis, MA 02660

Eastham Conservation Office
    (508) 240–5971
    555 Old Orchard Road
    Eastham, MA 02642

Falmouth Natural Resources Department
(508) 457–2536
59 Town Hall Square
Falmouth, MA 02540

Harwich Conservation Commission
(508) 430–7506
Town Hall
732 Main Street
Harwich, MA 02645

Martha's Vineyard Land Bank Commission
(508) 627–7141
167 Main Street, P.O. Box 2057
Edgartown, MA 02539

Mashpee Conservation Office
(508) 539–1414
16 Great Neck Road North
Mashpee, MA 02649

Nantucket Conservation Foundation
(508) 228–2884
P.O. Box 13
Nantucket, MA 02554

Sandwich Conservation Department
(508) 888–4200
16 Jan Sebastion Drive, Box 8
Sandwich, MA 02563

Sheriff's Meadow Foundation
(508) 693–5207
R.R.#1, Box 319X
Vineyard Haven, MA 02568

Truro Conservation Commission
(508) 349–3656
Town Hall
Town Hall Road, P.O. Box 2030
Truro, MA 02666

Wellfleet Conservation Commission
(508) 349–0300
Town Hall
300 Main Street
Wellfleet, MA 02667

Yarmouth Conservation Commission
(508) 398–2231
Town Hall
1146 Route 28
South Yarmouth, MA 02664

Yarmouth Conservation Trust
(508) 362–8270
P.O. Box 376
Yarmouth Port, MA 02675

Getting Ready

Use your common sense to select clothing for these excursions. Footwear demands the most attention. You'll want sturdy-but-comfortable, flat-soled shoes (a solid pair of sneakers would be sufficient for most of the walks). On longer treks, particularly the ones through soft sand, you should consider over-the-ankle shoes or boots to give extra support and keep sand out of your socks.

None of the walks call for specialized clothing beyond that already mentioned. We suggest wearing loose-fitting, comfortable clothes geared to the season and weather you're hiking in.

For the longer walks such as Sandy Neck and Great Island, you'll want to put more thought into preparations. You'd be wise to start early in the day to avoid the summer sun. Your trip will be much more enjoyable if you also carry a supply of water with you.

Caution . . .

There are only four real "dangers" to Cape and Islands walkers. All four of these can usually be avoided by taking some of the following precautions.

Too much sun can burn you and possibly cause sunstroke. Schedule the few longer walks in this book for early morning to avoid the midday sun's intense heat. Take hats and protective lotion with you even on the shorter hikes that briefly expose you to the sun.

Poison ivy grows abundantly on dunes and in wooded areas along many of these walks. It can be an erect shrub, a trailing vine, or a climber. Its three leaves may be shiny or dull, green or red, coarsely toothed or smooth-edged. Learn to recognize the plant and avoid it and anything that comes in contact with it.

A walk on any of these trails may acquaint you (and/or your dog) with two other Cape Cod and the Islands residents: the deer tick *(Ixodes dammini),* which may transmit Lyme disease, and the common American dog tick *(Dermacentor variabilis),* which may carry other diseases, including the less common Rocky Mountain Spotted Fever.

Lyme disease, named for the town in Connecticut where it was first recognized in 1975, is caused by corkscrew-shaped bacteria called spirochetes, which are transmitted to people by the bite of the pinhead-size deer tick. All stages of the deer tick (larva, nymph, and adult) bite humans. People bitten by a tick carrying Lyme disease may or may not develop a characteristic "bull's-eye" rash. Flu-like symptoms, including chills, fever, fatigue, headache, nausea, muscle and joint pain, and swollen glands, are common within a week to a month. Later symptoms, which may not occur until up to a year after the tick bite, include arthritis, meningitis, and neurological and cardiac problems. Timely treatment with antibiotics can cure the disease or lessen the severity of later complications. Therefore, if you are bitten by a tick or if you develop any of these symptoms, it is very important to see a doctor and mention the possibility of Lyme disease. Both Lyme disease and Rocky Mountain Spotted Fever are treated with antibiotics. The following preventive measures can reduce your chances of being bitten by a tick:

1. Tuck your pant legs into your socks. Tuck your shirt into your pants. This will help keep the ticks on the outside of your clothes where they can be readily seen and removed.
2. Wear light-colored clothing. The dark-colored ticks are more visible on this light background.
3. While walking, check your clothes often for ticks.
4. Apply insect repellents (according to label instructions) to shoes, socks, cuffs, and pant legs.
5. When you return from a walk, check—or have someone else check—your head and body thoroughly for ticks.

If you find a tick embedded in your skin, remove it by gently pulling it off with tweezers, being careful not to squeeze or crush it. Wash your hands afterward. Save the tick to show the doctor.

The annoying attack of other kinds of insects, such as mosquitoes or biting flies, can take the fun out of any walk, especially those passing through or near woods or swampy areas. Keep a good repellent handy just in case.

Rules and Regulations

Rules and regulations have been developed to help us preserve natural areas and the wildlife living there. Many areas have posted signs and printed literature detailing "dos and don'ts" that should be adhered to. Please remember the following while walking:

Stay on marked trails.
Camp, cook, hunt, and fish only where permitted.
Don't cut trees, branches, or flowers.
Keep dogs on a leash.
Carry small plastic bags to clean up after your dog.
Carry out empty what you carried in full.
Take only pictures.

Fees

Various admission, parking, and other fees associated with these properties may change at any time, without notice. While we endeavor to keep current, some fees may even change between book updating time and printing time. Fees currently less than $1.00 have been denoted as "nominal."

Cape Cod

Ashumet Holly
and Wildlife Sanctuary

Wampanoag Indians, in their customary manner of selecting names based on special attributes, called this area Ashumet, meaning "at or near a spring." Owned and operated by the Massachusetts Audubon Society, the Ashumet Holly and Wildlife Sanctuary offers an abundance of natural features as well as trail options.

The late Wilfrid Wheeler was foremost among many dedicated individuals who created splendid horticultural collections at the sanctuary. He gathered holly trees from all over the Cape, the islands, and other New England locations, and he developed winter-hardy strains from some of the older trees still growing in the sanctuary.

Mr. and Mrs. Josiah K. Lilly III purchased Wilfrid Wheeler's property after his death in 1961 and donated the unique, forty-nine-acre collection to the Massachusetts Audubon Society. Varieties of Oriental and European hollies and other native plants grow here.

You'll want to refer to a copy of the sanctuary's official trail map and interpretive brochure before deciding your route(s). Wooden posts and metal trail markers identify interpretive stations and other features explained in trail booklets. In true

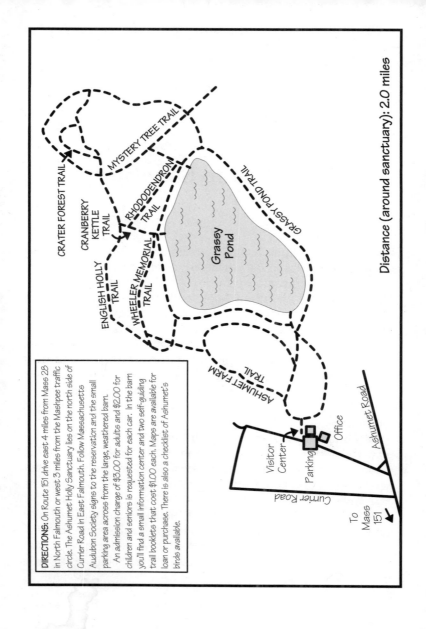

CRATER FOREST TRAIL

MYSTERY TREE TRAIL

CRANBERRY KETTLE TRAIL

RHODODENDRON TRAIL

ENGLISH HOLLY TRAIL

WHEELER MEMORIAL TRAIL

Grassy Pond

GRASSY POND TRAIL

ASHUMET FARM TRAIL

Visitor Center

Parking

Office

Ashumet Road

Currier Road

To Mass 151

DIRECTIONS: On Route 151 drive east 4 miles from Mass 28 in North Falmouth or west 3 miles from the Mashpee traffic circle. The Ashumet Holly Sanctuary lies on the north side of Currier Road in East Falmouth. Follow Massachusetts Audubon Society signs to the reservation and the small parking area across from the large, weathered barn.

An admission charge of $3.00 for adults and $2.00 for children and seniors is requested for each car. In the barn you'll find a small information center and two self-guiding trail booklets that cost $1.00 each. Maps are available for loan or purchase. There is also a checklist of Ashumet's birds available.

Distance (around sanctuary): 2.0 miles

Wampanoag fashion, the many trail names identify each area's significant characteristics.

The Mystery Tree Trail immediately arouses your curiosity. Look for the Japanese umbrella pine here. It is thought to be the only surviving species of a plant group that became extinct long ago. Watch also for the Ben Franklin Flowering Tree. Discovered in 1770 by botanist John Bartram along the Altamaha River in Georgia, these wild plants had disappeared by 1790 and no other wild plants of Franklinia have ever been found.

The Wheeler Memorial Trail pays tribute to Wilfrid Wheeler, the first commissioner of agriculture for Massachusetts. Nicknamed "the Holly Man," he propagated trees from cuttings and also moved wild trees to Ashumet, where originally no hollies existed. The sanctuary contains eight different species and sixty-five varieties of holly trees.

The Grassy Pond Trail leads around one of the 300 kettle ponds on Cape Cod. Melting glacial ice combined with the sedimentary buildup of sand and gravel and the bottom-sealing settling of finely ground soil or clay to form these kettle-shaped basins. You're apt to see glimpses of pond life along this route. During dry weather, the semiaquatic ribbon snake frequents the muddy shore. You'll also see black bullheads, commonly called catfish, wriggling in the shallows in search of food among underwater plant stems.

Belted kingfishers chatter from their perches in overhanging pine branches along the pond trail. You also may see a painted turtle at the water's edge. Its dark upper shell contrasts sharply with vivid yellow and red head and neck markings. Usually found in shallow, weedy waters, it feeds mostly on plants. But sharp, bony jaws enable it to eat small animals, dead or alive.

All sanctuary trails are color-coded. Blue dots lead away from the parking area, white dots identify connecting trails, and yellow dots lead back.

2

Lowell Holly Reservation

An intriguing, well-kept network of trails laces the varied wood-lands of Lowell Holly Reservation, a property of the Trustees of Reservations. Actually a 130-acre peninsula, the reservation di-vides Wakeby Pond and Mashpee Pond—two of the largest fresh-water ponds on Cape Cod. In addition to hiking, this area encourages nature study, fishing, and picnicking.

Abbott Lawrence Lowell, president of Harvard University from 1909 to 1933, gave the property to the Trustees of Reservations in 1943. The reservation remains open to the public year-round, sunrise to sunset. The public parking lot is open 9:00 A.M. to 5:00 P.M. between Memorial Day and Columbus Day. A parking fee or boat landing charge of $6.00 is collected on holidays and weekends in summer. An annual boat permit is available from the warden, who is on duty on summer weekends and holidays.

The trail leads left through a clearing with picnic tables and bears right toward Wakeby Pond after passing two short spurs on the right. From the pond's edge turn left and continue straight at the fork just ahead, following the white, circular blazes.

Note the contrasting trees along this shady route: the smooth-barked beeches, the medium-smooth hollies (with sharp-tipped leaves), and the rougher pitch pines. The way bends sharply left and reaches a fork just before the pond's shore. Go right. Listen for the calls of rufous-sided towhees *(drink-your-tea)*, gray catbirds (mewing calls), and common flickers *(flick or flicker)*. Flickers are

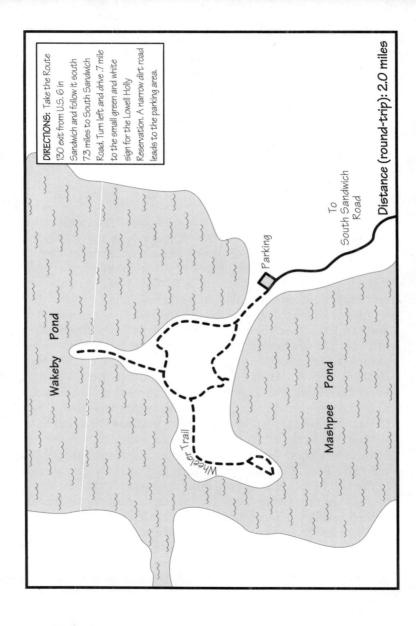

DIRECTIONS: Take the Route 130 exit from U.S. 6 in Sandwich and follow it south 7.3 miles to South Sandwich Road. Turn left and drive .7 mile to the small green and white sign for the Lowell Holly Reservation. A narrow dirt road leads to the parking area.

Wakeby Pond

Mashpee Pond

Wheeler Trail

Parking

To
South Sandwich
Road

Distance (round-trip): 2.0 miles

the only woodpeckers that commonly feed on the ground. They eat ants primarily, plus a variety of other insects and wild fruit. These brownish birds sport patches of bright yellow under tail and wing surfaces, red neck napes, and (in the male) a black mustache. Watch for their undulating flight and flashing white rumps.

Reaching another fork, follow the triangular white blazes left (circular white blazes lead right) onto the Wheeler Trail. Note the shade- and moisture-loving Solomon's seal to either side of the trail here. Tubular, greenish white flowers hang pendulously from between the leaves. Scars on its rootstock, likened to the seal of Solomon, give the plant its name. Each winter its arching, leafy stem dies, leaving a scar on the plant's root; thus, you can easily determine how old each plant is by counting the marks on the root.

After winding through stands of white pines, the path reaches another fork. Follow the arrows left for a loop walk over slightly elevated land. Occasional overlooks to Mashpee Pond appear through openings in the trees. Arriving back at the loop intersection, retrace your steps to the start of the Wheeler Trail and go left (following the white circles again).

Watch for multizoned polystictus growing on dead and downed trees through here. These pore fungi have leathery fans marked by varied, dull-colored bands. Due to their distinctive markings and shape, they have been nicknamed "turkey tails."

Reaching yet another fork, bear left onto the trail blazed with white squares. This path brings you out onto a narrow spit of land. Bushes pinch in from both sides before the way climbs a short grade and reaches a clearing. Although views are somewhat restricted by growing trees, you might hear the quacks of waterfowl on nearby waters.

Return to the most recent fork and swing sharply left, following white circles again. Passing large clusters of rhododendron and mountain laurel, the path nears the water once more.

The trail then dips into damp, shady areas overflowing with ferns before returning you to the intersection near the bar gate. Go left, back to the parking area.

If conditions are right, how about that picnic?

3

Ryder Conservation Lands

Native holly trees 50 feet high and 100 to 150 years old, fine stands of smooth-barked beeches, and towering pines that once attracted nesting eagles fill the Ryder Conservation Lands. The eagles are gone now, but other wildlife thrive in the natural cover throughout the sanctuary. A quiet stroll along the varied network of trails may bring you face to face with some of these wild creatures. Come prepared for swimming, boating, and fishing (Wakeby Pond boasts some of the finest Cape Cod freshwater fishing).

The Sandwich Conservation Commission acquired this 145-acre woodland and began developing it into a natural recreational area in the summer of 1975. The property now encompasses 243 acres. A modest entrance fee for the use of the beach parking area in season (June 15 to Labor Day) is charged to non–Sandwich residents.

Walk over the rise beyond the parking area and bear right off the road onto the trail. The needle-covered path winds through pines and oaks. Hollies abound through here. Mushrooms dot the trail at ankle height.

Go either way at the fork ahead. The left fork leads down through thick woods; the right one approaches Wakeby Pond and swings left along the water's edge to join the first a short distance ahead.

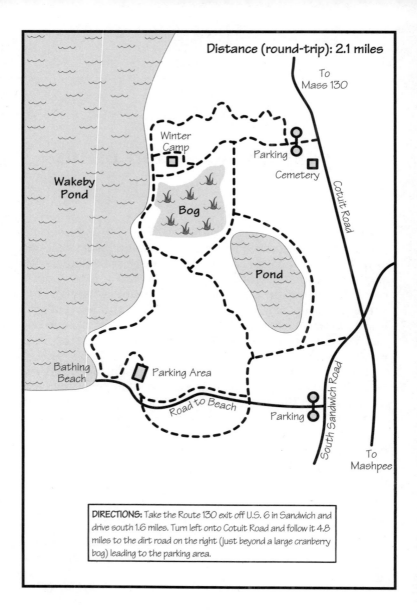

Distance (round-trip): 2.1 miles

To Mass 130

Winter Camp

Parking

Cemetery

Cotuit Road

Wakeby Pond

Bog

Pond

Bathing Beach

Parking Area

Road to Beach

Parking

South Sandwich Road

To Mashpee

DIRECTIONS: Take the Route 130 exit off U.S. 6 in Sandwich and drive south 1.6 miles. Turn left onto Cotuit Road and follow it 4.8 miles to the dirt road on the right (just beyond a large cranberry bog) leading to the parking area.

Take the next side trail on the left. It leads to a smaller clearing where you can sit and relax, refreshed by the breezes from Wakeby Pond.

Walk right from the clearing down to the Winter Camp. This completely rebuilt structure was formerly a screen house where harvested cranberries were dumped, separated, tested for soundness, and barreled.

Retrace your steps to the clearing and to the main trail next to the water. Swing left, through continuing beeches, to an open area near an old sluiceway (the wide trail entering from the left will be your return route to your car).

Go straight along the dike at the water's edge, past the old cranberry bog. The path soon splits above a depression. Go right for a walk through a heavily forested area. Once again, beeches predominate. The small, triangular beech nuts provide nourishment for the quail, raccoons, deer, rabbits, and squirrels who live here.

The trail reaches a clearing near a tiny cove. Turn left from the clearing onto a wider path and follow its looping route to a parking area. Go straight through the parking lot to the entrance road and turn left. Follow it .35 mile to the trail leading left.

This shady route passes down through oaks, beeches, and hollies to junction with a wider trail. Go left to a small clearing and continue on the trail leading straight ahead. This path meanders past a secluded five-acre pond that was once used as a nursery for otters. Today it provides an ideal habitat for a variety of waterfowl.

The soft, spongy path passes through towering maples before reaching the fork above the depression. Bear right, cross the dike, and follow the wide path .25 mile back to the parking area.

The Old Briar Patch

If I should walk in Gully Lane
Think you that I would find
The boyhood lost so long ago
The youth I left behind?
Are still the days so carefree there?
So filled with simple joy?
So heedless of the march of time
As when I was a boy.
Would clutching hands of bramble bush
Still reach to hold me fast
Or would thou treat me as a ghost—
A vision from the past?
Would summer berries taste as sweet?
The wild grapes spice the air
With quite the winey fragrance that
In memory haunts me there?

Ah me! So many years have fled
And mingled joy with pain
I fear to seek the boy who once
Did walk in Gully Lane.

Thornton W. Burgess reflects upon both his boyhood days in the
Gully Lane area and the wide-eyed enthusiasm that all too often

Distance (round-trip): 2.0 miles

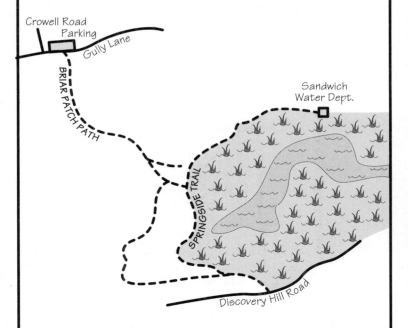

Crowell Road Parking

Gully Lane

BRIAR PATCH PATH

Sandwich Water Dept.

SPRINGSIDE TRAIL

Discovery Hill Road

DIRECTIONS: Turn south onto Chipman Road from Route 6A, either 1.1 miles east of the Sandwich Police Department or 2.3 miles west of the East Sandwich Post Office. At the road's end turn left onto Crowell Road. Follow it to the end and turn left onto Gully Lane. Park beside the split-rail fence 150 feet ahead.

disappears as we "mature" into grown-up society. Noted author of seventy children's books and 15,000 bedtime stories, Burgess was born in Sandwich in 1874. His love of nature and the foundation for his stories originated in the woodland now called the Old Briar Patch. The people of Sandwich sponsored this attractive, fifty-seven-acre area in 1974 in honor of Mr. Burgess.

You're likely to see many of the fabled Burgess characters somewhere within the Old Briar Patch. Watch and listen for Sammy Jay, Peter and Mrs. Rabbit, Reddy Fox, Old Mr. Toad, Jimmy Skunk, Johnny Chuck, Hooty Owl, Bobby Coon, and maybe even Paddy Beaver. Take time to look, listen, smell—and recapture those awakened memories of earlier days.

Bullbriers proliferate near the trail's starting point, providing ideal living areas for Peter and Mrs. Rabbit. The large, leathery leaves are rounded or heart-shaped. Numerous strong prickles along the stems offer protected hiding places for cottontail rabbits.

The way passes through two old stone walls. One wonders how this land used to look before early settlers spent backbreaking hours clearing trees and stones to prepare fields for farming.

After passing through a grove of deeply furrowed black locust trees, the path dips down to a swampy area and intersects the Springside Trail. Turn right and meander through shady beeches to the signed trail junction ahead. Turn sharply right and climb the moderate grade up Discovery Hill. Watch for the nervous movements of chipmunks in the stone wall to your left. Listen for the *bobwhite* call of quail from the field beyond.

Flattening out, the trail tops Discovery Hill and leads into a secluded clearing ringed by gigantic eastern white pines. Rustic benches encourage you to enjoy this private spot and perhaps reflect upon the message in Thornton Burgess's poem.

Twisting and turning, the trail returns you to the intersection near the swampy area. Swing down to the Springside Trail and go left for a cooling walk as far as the Sandwich Water Department building. Thick grapevines crowd this section of trail.

Return to the swamp intersection and go right onto Briar Patch Path. Retrace your original route to your starting point.

5

Talbot's Point
Conservation Lands

Talbot's Point protrudes into the Great Marsh surrounding Scornton Creek. Numerous bowers along the peninsula's edge encourage pauses for marsh watching. Green waves of wind-tossed grasses, peacefulness pierced only by wildlife activity, and rich, earthy smells are some of the natural tranquilizers to be discovered along the way.

Take the left trail from the clearing (through pitch pines) and bear right at the fork. Pass into a huge stand of red pines. There's a noticeable stillness to this area. Keeping the red pines on your left, cut right to the main trail. Then swing left.

Mourning doves may startle you with whistling wings as they take flight at your approach. Note their bulbous bodies, pointed wings, and tapered tails. When they walk, their heads bob with each step.

The trail is actually an old road. Unpainted birdhouses dot occasional trees and blend well with the surroundings.

Take the second side trail to the left (a trail opposite goes right). It leads quickly to a marsh overlook where you can see the state game farm. Ten thousand quail are raised there annually.

There are frequent views of the marsh as the trail swings right, still close to the marsh's edge. Rabbits find ideal habitats in the thick, trailside briers.

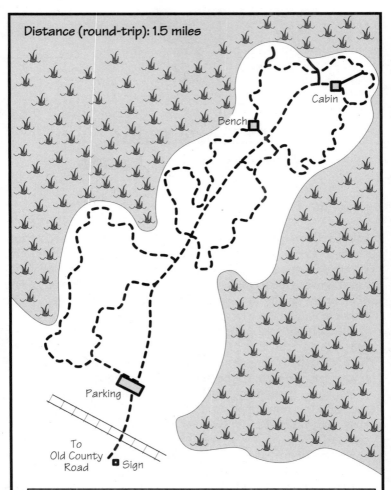

Distance (round-trip): 1.5 miles

Cabin

Bench

Parking

To
Old County
Road ■ Sign

DIRECTIONS: Turn south onto Old County Road opposite the East Sandwich Post Office on Route 6A. After 1.4 miles turn left onto a wide, sandy road. Cross the railroad tracks and park in the small cleared area. Dr. and Mrs. Fritz B. Talbot gave this land to the Sandwich Conservation Commission in 1963. Camping and open fires are not permitted here.

At a clearing a short trail leads right to the main trail. But go left here, continuing along the marsh's edge. Enjoy a rest and a marsh view at the rough-hewn bench in the clearing ahead.

Walk through thicker pine woods on a needled trail. Make sure you stay on the path—this area is loaded with poison ivy.

Continue through bare-branched pines to another clearing with a spur leading left and a short path leading right to the main trail. Stay straight here, circling around the point's perimeter. The trail curves back toward the open area. Go left at the fork ahead and left again at a second fork.

This damp area teems with ferns. After curling along the marsh's border, the path eventually enters pine woods. In late spring you may surprise a ruffed grouse. If accompanied by chicks, the hen will go into her broken-wing act to entice you away from the young.

When she has successfully diverted the danger, she'll thunder into the air and return to her chicks.

Eventually, this path rejoins the main trail directly opposite the original side trail you took. Go left onto the main trail and then right onto the next side trail.

This path winds beside the red pine woods. Look through openings on the right across cranberry bogs to the game farm's pheasant enclosures. Pass through a beech forest, climb a slight rise, and walk ahead to the parking area.

6

Sandy Neck

However you look at them, the sand dunes at Sandy Neck are impressive. They are 6.2 miles long, from 200 yards to .5 mile wide, and more than 4,000 years old. Ranging from flats to minimountains, the dunes look like angry waves on a storm-tossed sea.

Sheltered in Sandy Neck's southerly lee, the 3,000-acre Great Marshes began to form some 3,500 years ago. Today the marshes support an extensive chain of marine life and provide protection and food for both sea and land birds.

The vastness of these traditional Cape Cod natural features will awe you as you walk through Sandy Neck. Come prepared for hiking, swimming, sunbathing, beachcombing, bird-watching, and fishing.

This hike's route passes through soft sand, the sun can become unbearably hot, and there is little shelter along the way. Only persons in excellent physical condition should attempt this trek. Make sure you have water, suntan lotion, sturdy footwear (preferably with ankle support), and a good knowledge of your route. Hike in the early morning to avoid the midday sun (and increase your chances of seeing wildlife).

Walk .25 mile back down the entrance road (past the attendant's booth at the four-wheel-drive entrance road) and turn left onto the sandy road along the marsh's edge. You'll see two non-chemical methods of insect control stretching across the marsh.

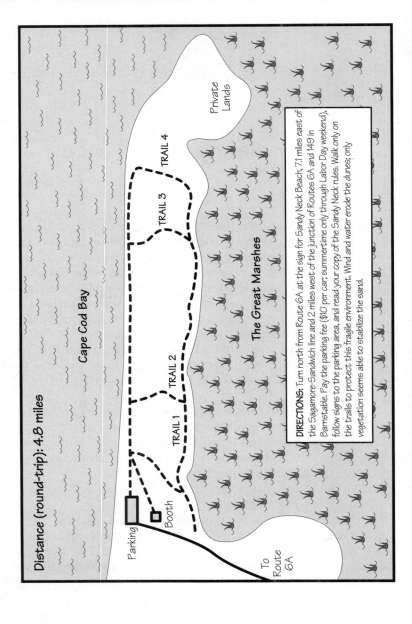

Distance (round-trip): 4.8 miles

Cape Cod Bay

Parking

Booth

To Route 6A

TRAIL 1

TRAIL 2

TRAIL 3

TRAIL 4

The Great Marshes

Private Lands

DIRECTIONS: Turn north from Route 6A at the sign for Sandy Neck Beach, 7.1 miles east of the Sagamore-Sandwich line and 2 miles west of the junction of Routes 6A and 149 in Barnstable. Pay the parking fee ($10 per car; summertime only through Labor Day weekend), follow signs to the parking area, and read your copy of the Sandy Neck rules. Walk only on the trails to protect this fragile environment. Wind and water erode the dunes; only vegetation seems able to stabilize the sand.

The raised wooden boxes attract greenhead (horse) flies, which enter from the bottom, become trapped, and die. The birdhouses attract tree swallows, which devour flying insects.

Your pace will slow in the heavy sand here. This is an ideal area, however, to look for animal signs. An animal-track book will help you identify deer, rabbits, and the host of other animals that frequent the area.

After approximately ¾ mile, you reach a large orange sign pointing left to Trail 1. Disregard the sign and continue straight as the trail curls along the marsh's edge. Orange markers guide your way. Watch for them at narrow forks (most of which rejoin the main trail quickly in any case).

After passing a small island of trees on the right, the road heads for a high, brush-covered dune and suddenly veers right around it. The setting is primitive and isolated.

Cedars and wild roses thicken the trailside ahead. This is an ideal spot to rest in the shade and scan the marsh for bird activity.

The way winds between two dwellings near the marsh, passes another on the left, and reaches the sign for Trail 2 after 2.25 miles. Go left between towering dunes. Turn left again onto Beach Road, which parallels the bay. Walking becomes easier atop the beach's pebbles and packed sand. A 1-mile walk along the beach brings you to the exit for Trail 1. If you're still feeling fresh, go left here and travel 1.25 miles back to your car. For a quicker return continue straight for .25 mile to the parking area.

7

Callery-Darling Conservation Area: Eastern Trail

The Callery-Darling Conservation Area is located in Yarmouth Port, a small, historic village on the north shore of central Cape Cod that features beaches, waterways, and marshes abutting expansive Cape Cod Bay. The Callery-Darling area, named after former owners of the land and a Yarmouth Conservation Trust member, contains nearly 2.5 miles of trails traversing diverse ecosystems and habitats. Saltwater marshes and freshwater streams and wetlands, thicket forest, beach, shaded woodlands, and remnants of old farm meadows support a wide array of waterfowl, such as the great blue heron, with a wingspan of nearly 6 feet; the marsh hawk; and various species of ducks, geese, and seagoing gulls. White-tailed deer and cottontail rabbits are prolific throughout the area, although deer, which are nocturnal feeders, are rarely seen during the daytime. You may see a red fox peering out from the thick underbrush or a scurrying muskrat heading to water.

The Eastern Trail (our name, for the purposes of distinguishing it from other Callery-Darling trails) begins at a grassy parking area on Alms House Road. At the head of the trail, marked by three wooden posts, a permanent trail map designates major points on the trails. Just past the map and a small bench, the trail forks left and right. Take the right trail, which in a minute or two will cross Center Street. Here the trail enters a steamy forest

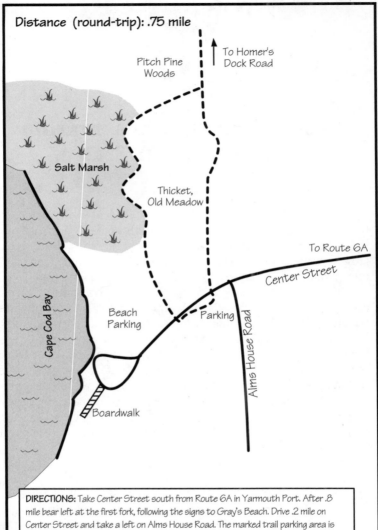

Distance (round-trip): .75 mile

Pitch Pine Woods

To Homer's Dock Road

Salt Marsh

Thicket, Old Meadow

To Route 6A

Center Street

Cape Cod Bay

Beach Parking

Parking

Alms House Road

Boardwalk

DIRECTIONS: Take Center Street south from Route 6A in Yarmouth Port. After .8 mile bear left at the first fork, following the signs to Gray's Beach. Drive .2 mile on Center Street and take a left on Alms House Road. The marked trail parking area is immediately on the right off Alms House Road.

of red cedar and oak trees, with a thick undergrowth of sweet pepperbush, fox grape, wintergreen, blueberry, bayberry, honeysuckle (in late summer, replete with red berries), and greenbrier, among other plants. If you look carefully, you may see the tiny, pink-flowered beach pea in a small, boggy wet area on the left. The growth in this area—once a meadow of a nineteenth-century farm—is so dense in places that the sun is nearly blocked.

The small, white triangles nailed to trees along the way are trail markers. Since the trails weave near and around residential areas, the markers are there to prevent you from entering private property.

After ten minutes you'll see a wooden post on your left where the trail forks left and straight. The straight section will bring you into an open area of pitch pine woodland, with homes visible in the distance. A few hundred feet beyond are a small parking area and the trail entrance on Homer's Dock Road.

The left branch moves quickly into overgrown brush forest again, yet through the thicket you can see open space. Within five minutes you'll be standing at the head of a salt marsh, dense with salt hay, cordgrass, cattails, and pathside ferns and bayberry, with red cedar and white oak behind. The seven birdhouses on poles on the marsh are meant to attract the tree swallow, which counts the greenhead fly as a favorite food.

The path skirts the marsh for a few minutes, and in places it can be mucky and slippery, particularly after a rain. It then bears left into the thicket again and finally empties onto—here's a pleasant surprise for the kids—a playground. This is Gray's Beach, a public area offering a boardwalk, toilets, a covered picnic area, and a beach: maybe just what you're looking for after a sweaty walk.

To return to the parking area, cross Center Street again and enter the trail on the right. A five-minute walk through brambles will see you back to your car.

Due to the trail's proximity to wetlands, mosquitoes, deerflies, and greenhead flies come out in early morning and evening in summer. A dose of a good repellent will help.

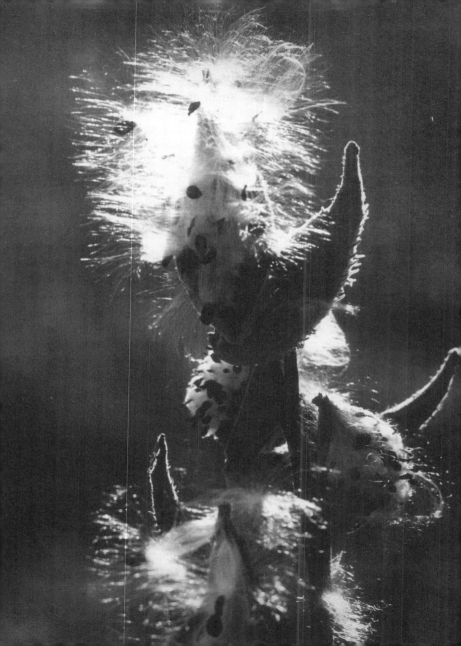

8

Callery-Darling Conservation Area: Western Trail

Quiet Yarmouth Port, a small Yarmouth village on the north shore of central Cape Cod, hosts the Callery-Darling Conservation Area. The Yarmouth Conservation Trust maintains and promotes the trails, along with six other conservation areas, for both ecological and recreational purposes. The Western Trail (our name, not the trust's) of the Callery-Darling area covers nearly 2 miles of trail systems darting in and out of residential areas, old cranberry bogs, saltwater marshes, freshwater streams and wetlands, and pine and thicket forests. The land supports a wide array of woodland birds, such as the ruffed grouse, the ring-tailed pheasant, and the common quail, as well as the water-loving and spindly great blue heron, the marsh hawk, and various species of ducks and geese. White-tailed deer and cottontail rabbits can be seen in the woods, although deer are rarely seen during the daytime.

The trail starts at a dirt road at the end of Alms House Road, taking you through a dense undergrowth of fox grape vines, blueberry, and other low bushes. It then enters a white oak forest (follow the white triangle markers nailed to trees). What appears to be a marsh on the left was once a cranberry bog; the cranberry industry has been one of the mainstays of the Cape Cod economy for more than two centuries. The erstwhile freshwater bog now

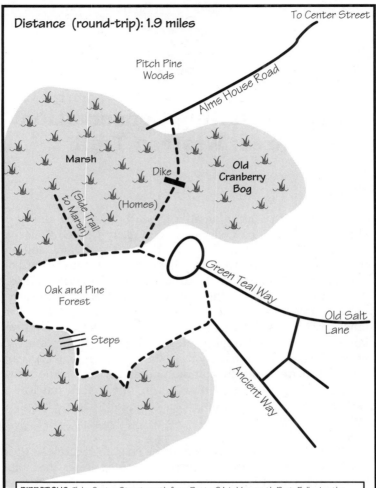

Distance (round-trip): 1.9 miles

To Center Street

Pitch Pine Woods

Alms House Road

Marsh

Dike

Old Cranberry Bog

(Side Trail to Marsh)

(Homes)

Oak and Pine Forest

Green Teal Way

Old Salt Lane

Steps

Ancient Way

DIRECTIONS: Take Center Street south from Route 6A in Yarmouth Port. Following the signs to Gray's Beach; look for Alms House Road on the left. Drive .2 mile to the end of the dirt road, where you'll see a trail sign. Parking here is limited, so you may want to park at the main trail lot at the eastern end of Alms House Road.

sports brackish water and is slowly being taken over by the vigorous reeds, grasses, and cattails of marshland vegetation. After a minute or two, you'll cross a small dike over the marsh, where the views are expansive. The blue boxes sitting on the grass are greenhead fly traps, set up by the Department of Natural Resources. Greenheads are particularly annoying on early summer mornings and evenings.

Soon the trail bears right into a winding path through a pitch pine and oak forest with an undergrowth of huckleberry, greenbrier, and bearberry. Pitch pine and scrub and white oak are well adapted to the sandy, acidic soils of seaside environs and are able to resist the salt-laden air. Note that the oaks are generally smaller than the pines. While the pines strive for sunlight, the white oaks can thrive in the shade. The pines will eventually die out, and the next generation of trees in this area will be oaks, a result of a process called plant succession. Several private homes are not too distant.

After a few minutes the trail will bear hard left, while a dirt-road section of the trail heads straight. Bear left, still in the pine forest but skirting a marsh on the right. You'll walk up some simple steps built into a small hillock. Bear left again, onto a dirt road, at the next major fork.

In a minute or two, you'll be at a T junction on the trail. Proceeding right will bring you to a small parking area at Ancient Way; heading left will bring you to Green Teal Way, a public road. Take the left road and walk a few hundred feet along it to the cul-de-sac. At the end of the cul-de-sac, on the left, is what appears to be a private driveway. You can walk up the driveway for access to the trail again. At the first fork, go right to retrace your steps to Alms House Road.

9

Yarmouth Historical Society Nature Trails

A wheel-shaped herb garden introduces you to the Historical Society of Old Yarmouth's Nature Trails. Rosemary (signifying remembrance) rises from the center. A trail guide is available at the Gate House for a nominal donation. It is keyed to cement markers along the trail and provides brief explanations of interesting botanical and geographical features.

Indians originally called this area Mattacheset, meaning "old or planting lands by the borders of the water." Here they planted beans, pumpkins, and corn in natural and man-made clearings. Deer and smaller game filled the forests, while ponds provided habitats for fish and waterfowl. There is little wonder that this naturally rich region was one of the first to be appropriated by white men.

Anthony Thacher, one of the three founders of Yarmouth, selected 156 acres of the best land for himself. He eventually paid the Indians with coats, breeches, hoes, hatchets, and metal kettles. Though Thacher descendants distinguished themselves in both the town and the larger world, they retained a love for the original land. In the early 1970s, a Thacher relative donated the present fifty-acre woodland tract to the Historical Society of Old Yarmouth, which continues to maintain it.

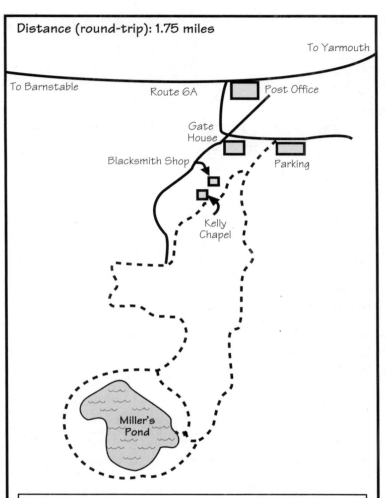

Distance (round-trip): 1.75 miles

To Yarmouth

To Barnstable

Route 6A

Post Office

Gate House

Blacksmith Shop

Parking

Kelly Chapel

Miller's Pond

DIRECTIONS: Turn south from Route 6A onto the road leading behind the Yarmouth Port Post Office. Drive the short distance to the parking area near the Gate House. A nominal charge covers the cost of admission and a descriptive pamphlet. Dogs must be on a leash. The trails are open year-round. Trail maps are available at the Gate House; a small donation is appreciated.

The sandy trail begins to the left of the wheel-shaped herb garden. It quickly branches left and follows a grassy swath cut through open fields. The way leads into a quiet area forested with pitch pine, the Cape's most common pine. It generally grows on poor soil and can withstand strong winds and salt spray.

Oaks begin to mix with the pines. Delicate, pink lady's slippers dot the trailsides at ground level. A member of the orchid family, the flower can be easily identified by the singular, puffed-out, pink petal resembling the toe of a slipper. Two oval leaves from 6 to 8 inches long grow from the base of the stalk. Each plant has only one flower and one stem. Laws prohibit the picking of these flowers.

The stillness of the young oak forest might be broken by rustlings in the leaves: possibly from a chipmunk or squirrel, but more probably from a rufous-sided towhee. Its unmistakable call is a slurred *chewink*. Its large size (up to 8 inches), dark head, rusty sides, white belly, and large white spots at the corners of its long, rounded tail make this bird easily identifiable. Towhees feed almost exclusively on the ground, persistently scratching away dead leaves to get at the insects underneath.

Step down over the log-supported stairway to Miller's Pond. You can turn left and enjoy the .5-mile Pond Trail, which circles the wetland area; or right, taking the short spur to the water's edge at marker 9. You may see animal tracks as well as frogs and turtles from this tiny observation area. Migrating waterfowl feed here in spring and fall.

Return to the main trail and follow it along the eastern shore. Pine odors engulf you as you weave your way through upland woods.

The path swings right at the old chapel and blacksmith shop and leads back to the parking area.

10

John Wing Trail

The natural creation of a salt marsh like the one skirting Wing's Island requires the life and death of a continuing succession of plants and marine life for hundreds of years. When a salt marsh is destroyed, it cannot be artificially reconstructed. The town of Brewster's diligent efforts have preserved the natural loveliness of Wing's Island's 140 acres of upland, beach, and salt marsh.

The trail begins 100 feet west of the Cape Cod Museum of Natural History's parking lot. An attractive signboard displays a map and capsule history of Wing's Island. Remember to *check times for high tides* before starting your hike because the causeway becomes flooded, particularly during spring tides. You might consider wearing waterproof boots on this walk.

There are a fair amount of poison ivy along the trail and a high population of dog ticks, *Dermacentor variabilis,* in this area. (Remember to check yourself for ticks.)

Hike between a dense tree and shrub arborway before emerging into the openness of the salt marsh.

The short, soft, salt marsh hay flourishing in the Wing's Island environs was of agricultural importance to Brewster's earlier residents. They piled the seasonal cuttings of marsh hay onto horse-drawn wagons and took them to the island itself, where they laid the hay out to dry. Later, local farmers carted it away to store in their barns for cattle feed and mulch or to

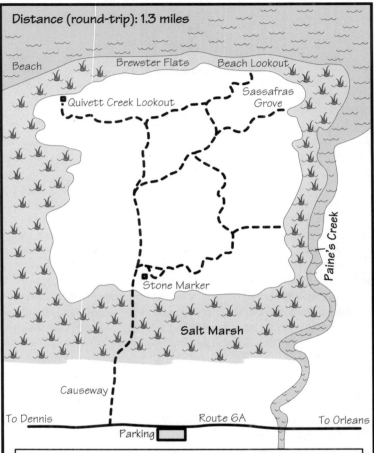

Distance (round-trip): 1.3 miles

Beach

Brewster Flats

Beach Lookout

Quivett Creek Lookout

Sassafras Grove

Paine's Creek

Stone Marker

Salt Marsh

Causeway

To Dennis

Route 6A

To Orleans

Parking

DIRECTIONS: To reach the start of the trail on the north side of Route 6A, drive 2.4 miles east of the intersection of Route 134 and 6A in Dennis or 1.6 miles west of the intersection of Mass 137 and 6A in Brewster. Turn south into the John Wing Trail parking area (across the street from the Cape Cod Museum of Natural History). Remember—there are no public rest rooms at the John Wing Trail. Use the ones at the Brewster Police and Fire station 2 miles to the east. The John Wing Trail Guide, a fifteen-page pamphlet with descriptions keyed to the trail's interpretive markers, is available for a nominal fee at the Brewster Conservation Department or the Cape Cod Museum of Natural History.

spread around the foundations of their homes for insulation.

After crossing the causeway the trail reaches the more elevated island, where thick vegetation narrows the way. Stay straight; do not take the path that enters from the right.

Keep left at two quick forks ahead as you head toward Quivett Creek Lookout. The path descends a bit, then arrives at a clearing at the marsh's edge. By remaining as quiet and hidden as possible, you may be able to watch stalking blue herons, acrobatic tree swallows, and hovering marsh hawks.

Retrace your steps to the most recent fork in the trail and go left toward Beach Lookout. Pitch pines shade both hikers and bearberry beneath them. Turn left as another trail joins from the right. From this vantage point you overlook the Brewster Flats and the beach in the distance.

Return to the most recent fork and stay straight. At the next fork go left, following the twisting trail that passes through a sassafras grove just before reaching the salt marsh edge. The untoothed sassafras leaves may be three-fingered or mitten- or egg-shaped. Spring-blooming, greenish yellow flowers and autumn-ripening, small blue fruits aid identification. Settlers once fashioned barrels, posts, and dugout canoes from the tree's durable, coarse lumber; they boiled the roots and bark to make sassafras tea, their "spring tonic."

Return to the most recent trail junction and go left, and left again at a quick fork. Staying straight at the fork ahead, you reach the stone marking the site of John Wing's home on the left. Just beyond the stone rejoin the original trail, turn left, and return to Route 6A.

11

Cape Cod Museum
of Natural History:
North Trail

An exciting, educational experience awaits you at the Cape Cod Museum of Natural History and its two trails: the North Trail (described here) and the South Trail (Walk 12). In addition to the trails, the museum provides natural history exhibits, live animal exhibits, films, lectures, classes for adults and children, and a fine environmental reference library. The museum is open from 9:30 A.M. to 4:30 P.M. Monday through Saturday and from 11:00 A.M. to 4:30 P.M. Sunday. Admission fees are adults thirteen to sixty-four years, $5.00; seniors sixty-five and over, $4.50; children five to twelve years, $2.00; children under five years, free.

Enter the museum from the parking lot and be prepared to spend some time discovering new aspects of the natural world. Skeletons and stuffed specimens let you study the "ins and outs" of nature's inhabitants at close range. Dioramas and aquariums display animals in nature-like settings. More than 5,000 books and periodicals about natural history fill the shelves of the museum's Clarence Hay Library. Special education programs take place in the auditorium, and the museum's store features an array of nature- and science-related gifts and books.

Pick up a guide to the North Trail at the museum and step

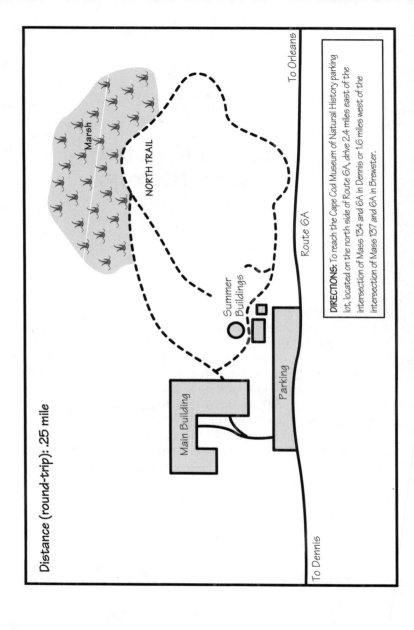

Distance (round-trip): .25 mile

Main Building

Parking

Summer Buildings

NORTH TRAIL

Marsh

Route 6A

To Dennis

To Orleans

DIRECTIONS: To reach the Cape Cod Museum of Natural History parking lot, located on the north side of Route 6A, drive 2.4 miles east of the intersection of Mass 134 and 6A in Dennis or 1.6 miles west of the intersection of Mass 137 and 6A in Brewster.

outside from the museum's lower level. Numbered stations along this nature trail will help you identify much of the flora native to Cape Cod. Follow the path as it leads toward the marsh.

Watch immediately for wild roses. Not to be confused with the larger *Rosa rugosa* (wrinkled rose) that is abundant on the Cape, this dark pink, medium-size rose has downward-curving thorns. Its flowers supply nectar for numerous insects.

The worn path leads along the marsh edge and reaches a short boardwalk. Walk out onto the large rock at the creek's edge for a better view of the area. The salt marsh cordgrass bordering the edges of the creek grows where salinity is high. It thrives in sand flats, where its roots are submerged only half the time.

Just before the path dips into thicker growth, look left at the cattails. The slender, brown "cat's tail" is actually thousands of tiny female flowers topped by a lighter-colored spike containing the male flowers. Cattails play vital roles within the marsh ecosystem. Muskrats eat their roots and stems and use them for construction materials, nesting birds and ducks seek their protective cover, and the ever-present red-winged blackbirds perch on their slender stems.

The path leads into thicker growth dominated by sumacs. Two kinds, both nonpoisonous, are evident here. Both have the typical sumac leaves made up of eleven or more toothed leaflets. Dwarf sumac has narrow wings along the leafstalk between shiny leaflets; smooth sumac has hairless twigs and leafstalks with no wings.

The shady trail passes beneath a stand of tupelos and soon after reaches a bench where you can relax while looking out across the marsh. Turn left at the bench to follow the original path back to the museum.

12

Cape Cod Museum of Natural History: South Trail

During its passage through marshland and upland forest, the South Trail passes over Paine's Creek, a major migration route for alewives. Known as herring on Cape Cod, alewives make an annual spring migration from the ocean to inland rivers and streams to lay their eggs. A single female may carry as many as 60,000 to 100,000 eggs. Pilgrims sometimes depended on alewives as an extra food source and also used them to fertilize cornfields. Today conservation measures keep alewives from being overfished and allow them to reach their spring spawning grounds.

Pick up your trail guide at the museum information desk.

From the parking lot you can see the South Trail's sign across Route 6A. (You can walk directly from the parking lot, but you'll miss the numerous interesting features within the museum complex.)

Leave traffic sounds behind by stepping down over wooden steps into the cooling shade of shadbush and highbush blueberry. The path leads out to a marsh area and crosses a couple of wooden bridges over sluiceways.

These sluiceways once controlled the draining and flooding of the area to the right, which used to be a cranberry bog. Native

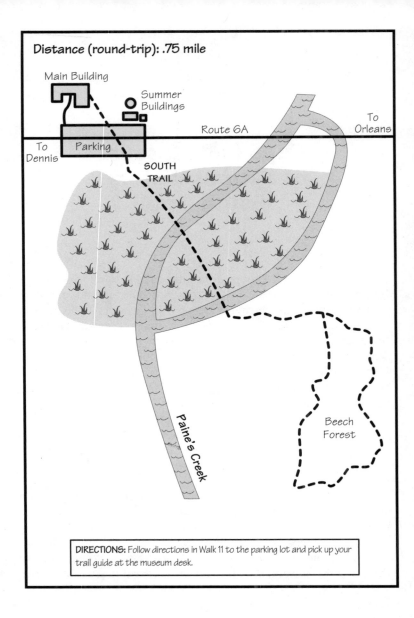

Distance (round-trip): .75 mile

Main Building

Summer Buildings

Route 6A

To Orleans

To Dennis

Parking

SOUTH TRAIL

Paine's Creek

Beech Forest

DIRECTIONS: Follow directions in Walk 11 to the parking lot and pick up your trail guide at the museum desk.

Americans colored rugs and blankets with cranberry juice and flavored pemmican cakes and succotash with its tartness. Pilgrim women used the native fruit in cooking and cheered up their wardrobes with the crimson pigment. Both Native Americans and the early settlers believed in the fruit's healing powers. Wampanoag Indians of Cape Cod treated poison arrow wounds with a cranberry poultice. They also imbibed the juice to calm their nerves. Rich in vitamin C, cranberries helped prevent scurvy among early American seamen voyaging to distant ports.

As you continue along the dike and into the woods ahead, watch for bird and animal life. You're apt to see deer, raccoons, muskrats, and a variety of birds. Animal tracks and "signs" (such as a discarded snake skin or droppings) will make this part of the walk all the more interesting.

Cross the large footbridge over Paine's Creek and enter the hardwood forest. The way leads through beech and tupelo groves before bending right beside a split-rail fence. Occasional orange wooden arrows guide you around this circuit portion of the walk. Trailsides teem with poison ivy.

Nearing the end of the circuit, you arrive at a huge boulder sitting above a sand hole. It's fun to imagine Native Americans crouching behind this glacial erratic and looking out over the expanses of marsh for animal—or perhaps human—movement.

The path swings right to rejoin the original trail. Turn left and retrace your steps back to Route 6A.

13

Stoney Brook Mill Sites

Early Cape Cod settlers used both wind- and water-powered gristmills to grind corn for bread. When a stream, brook, or river with a year-round flow of water was discovered, a miller was granted water rights and free labor was provided to help build a gristmill. A dam was built, and the resulting millpond delivered a steady flow of water to move the wheel. Mills became centers of gossip and information, as everyone stopped at one time or another to have corn ground.

You can watch corn being ground and packaged for sale at the Stoney Brook Gristmill on selected afternoons in July and August (call 508–896–1734 for schedules). There is also a free-admission museum upstairs. At any time you can meander through the lovely grounds behind the mill. A millpond, dam, and herring run nestle within the tranquil, flowered setting.

A short, bricked-in path to the right of the mill leads up to the millpond. A split-rail fence and sprawling honeysuckle vines surround this serene body of water. In spring and early summer, the sweet-smelling honeysuckle blossoms perfume the air. Yellow and white trumpet-shaped flowers bloom from April through July; blackberries appear in August.

Look down into the still waters for sunfish activity. The 4- to 6-inch green sunfish spawn in colonies. Males push aside pond bottom vegetation and fan shallow, saucer-shaped nests in the

Distance (round-trip): .25 mile

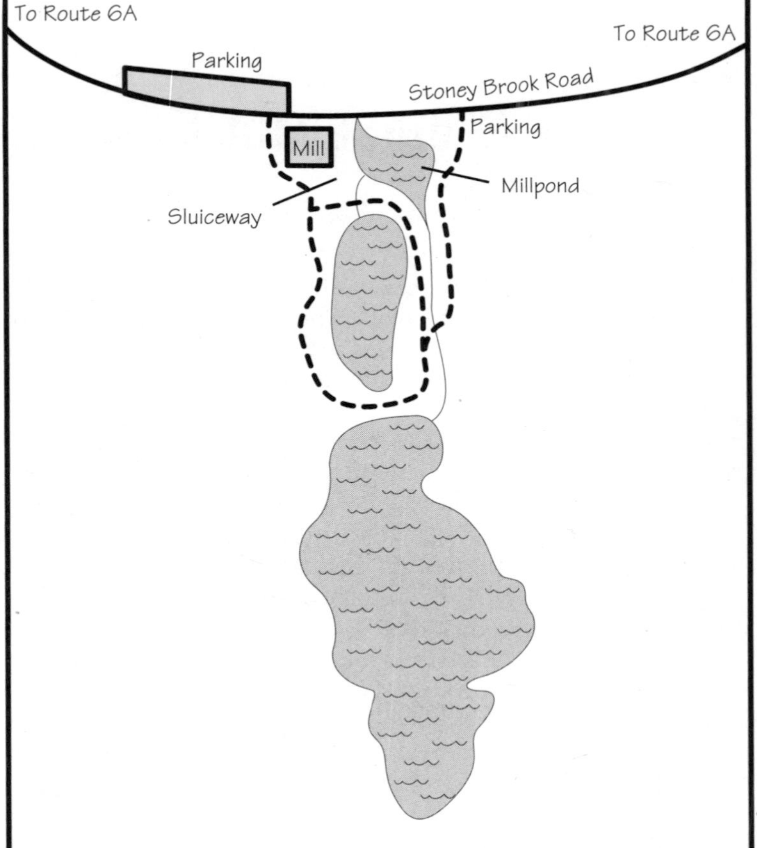

To Route 6A

To Route 6A

Parking

Stoney Brook Road

Parking

Mill

Millpond

Sluiceway

DIRECTIONS: On Route 6A in Brewster, turn south onto Stoney Brook Road at the flashing yellow light located 3.3 miles east of the junction of 6A and 134 in Dennis and .7 mile west of the junction of 6A and 137 in Brewster. Drive .7 mile to the mill (on the left). Parking is available across the street.

sand with their fins. You'll see these residual signs of spawning activity throughout the year.

Wind your way up toward the larger pond and cross the footbridges. A sluicegate regulates the flow of water from the upper pond down to the mill itself.

Beyond the second footbridge sounds of rushing water draw you beneath drooping weeping willows to the stone and cement sluiceway. In spring you'll see thousands of tiny fish sashaying in the turbulent waters. These young alewives ("fry") hatch in the upper pond and, when about an inch long, begin their journey down Stoney Brook to the ocean. In three to four years, they will migrate back to spawn themselves.

This is a good spot to sit on a stone wall and enjoy the tranquil setting. The privacy of the secluded glen is highlighted by thick tree and shrub growth and broken only by the quieting sounds of rushing water and occasional croaking of frogs. A camera will help you remember this peaceful area.

At the fork ahead go left to complete the loop around the lower pond. When back at this junction, go right, alongside the tumbling stream, toward the road.

You'll have a close-up view of the mill from across the small pond. This is a good vantage point from which to watch the water move the wheel as it, in turn, supplies the power for the grinding apparatus.

A few steps more will return you to Stoney Brook Road. Cross over and take the walk along the "ladders" where the herring come up in the spring. Go over the bridge and back to Stoney Brook Road.

14

Harding's Beach

The more barren an area is, the more it attracts the horned lark. Each breeding pair appears to need some sparsely vegetated land within its territory. Thus, the scoured dunes along the Harding's Beach Trail are a favored horned lark haunt. When this bird is in flight, its white underparts contrast sharply with its black tail. The horned lark moves by walking, rather than hopping, across the sand. If disturbed, it will fly only briefly before returning to earth.

There is a walking trail here that was established by the Chatham Conservation Foundation, Inc., which also preserves other open areas, marshes, and uplands. Be aware that although the trail still exists, it is no longer maintained by the foundation. You may or may not be able to use the trail depending on how overgrown the vegetation around it is. If you can't use the trail, you can still make a delightful loop as indicated on the map. A copy of *A Beachcomber's Botany,* with essays and comments by Dr. Loren C. Petry and illustrations by Marcia Norman, will add greatly to your enjoyment of this area. Rights to the book were donated to the Chatham Conservation Foundation in 1972, and the proceeds, along with gifts and membership dues, enable the foundation to continue its valuable work.

If it is accessible, walk on the wide, sandy road that the trail follows for .6 mile. Numerous side trails shortcut between salt spray rose and beach plum to the beach on the right.

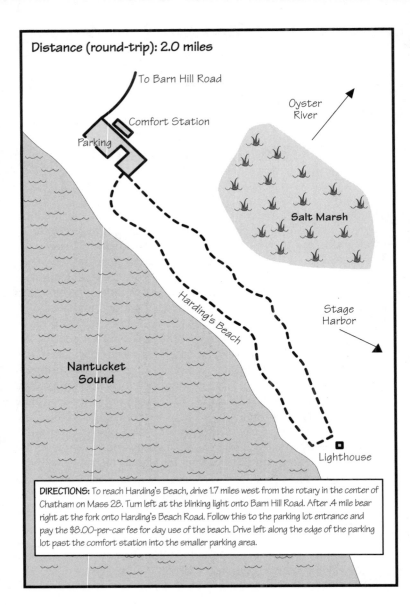

Distance (round-trip): 2.0 miles

To Barn Hill Road

Oyster River

Comfort Station

Parking

Salt Marsh

Harding's Beach

Stage Harbor

Nantucket Sound

Lighthouse

DIRECTIONS: To reach Harding's Beach, drive 1.7 miles west from the rotary in the center of Chatham on Mass 28. Turn left at the blinking light onto Barn Hill Road. After .4 mile bear right at the fork onto Harding's Beach Road. Follow this to the parking lot entrance and pay the $8.00-per-car fee for day use of the beach. Drive left along the edge of the parking lot past the comfort station into the smaller parking area.

The beach plum, a straggly, coastal shrub, bears purplish fruit used over the centuries to concoct sauces, preserves, pies, and jellies. Its white flowers bloom from April to June. Egg-shaped leaves, hairy buds, and velvety twigs will also help you identify this shrub.

Look left across the dunes to the salt marsh and Oyster River beyond. Fishermen grow and harvest oysters in this saltwater inlet; naturally flourishing bay scallops are also part of the bounty harvested there. (Chatham's early businesses included fishing, whaling, shipbuilding, and a saltworks.) You top a long, low grade and are treated to wide-ranging views of Oyster River, the salt marshes, and Stage Harbor to the left; look right to see Nantucket Sound and low, sandy Monomoy Island.

Continue straight to the lighthouse. You can turn left and walk back along the beautiful meadow or turn right and meander along the water's edge.

If you choose the water, your first ocean view may include a glimpse of the common tern's buoyant flight or rocketing dive. These birds fly parallel to the shore with bills pointed downward, ever scanning the shallows for schools of shiners. Black-capped and swallow-tailed, common terns plummet into the water to capture their prey. Diving terns are a positive sign for fishermen seeking bass and bluefish, for these game fish feed on shiners.

Take your shoes off, roll up your pant legs, and enjoy a cooling walk in the shallows of your return route. Stop to examine the assortment of shells—and seaweed and driftwood—awash on the beach. Molting adult horseshoe crabs deposit their shells upon the shore. (Actually, these animals are not crabs at all. Their closest relative became extinct 400 million years ago. This living fossil's closest relative today is the spider.) Though many bathers fear them, horseshoe crabs are harmless.

Complete your day at Harding's Beach with a swim or some surf casting.

15

Fort Hill Trail

Natural and local history blend as the Fort Hill Trail wanders over boardwalks through the Red Maple Swamp, crosses Skiff Hill, edges Nauset Marsh, ascends Fort Hill, and circles the Captain Edward Penniman House.

Pick up a Cape Cod National Seashore trail guide at the far end of the parking lot and step onto the wide trail. Take the left trail fork just ahead and descend over log-girdled steps. The path leads through meadows dotted with pines and cedars before entering the swamp.

Gray, weathered boardwalks curl through the lush vegetation. Narrow, scaly plates shingle the massive hulks of aged red maples that turn brilliant shades of gold and red. Cinnamon fern and wood fern proliferate in this damp, shady setting.

Ascend the paved path to Skiff Hill, where an octagonal, open-sided structure shelters Indian Rock. Nauset Indians used the boulder as a grinding rock, shaping bone points, fish hooks, sharpening tools, and weapons on its varied surfaces.

The shortcut to the right leads back to the parking lot, but there's more to see ahead. Leaving Skiff Hill, the trail curves through a forest of pine and cedar. On the way to Fort Hill, scan Nauset Marsh, where egrets, great blue herons, or other waterfowl might be observed.

Ascend the sloping path toward Fort Hill past a large glacial boulder. Early settlers probably used the spike driven into the

Distance (round-trip): 1.5 miles

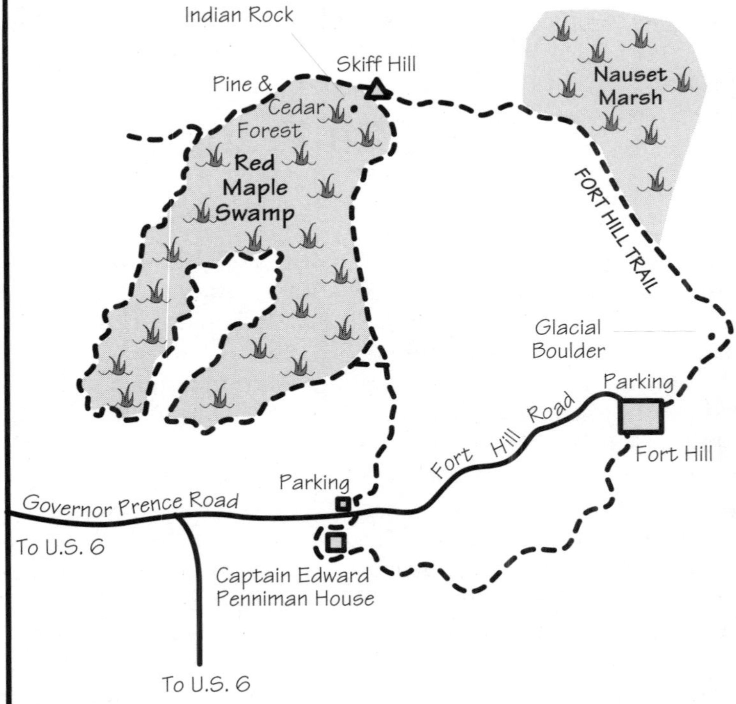

Indian Rock

Skiff Hill

Nauset Marsh

Pine & Cedar Forest

Red Maple Swamp

FORT HILL TRAIL

Glacial Boulder

Parking

Fort Hill Road

Fort Hill

Parking

Governor Prence Road

To U.S. 6

Captain Edward Penniman House

To U.S. 6

DIRECTIONS: Drive north for 1.2 miles on Route 6 from the rotary junction of U.S. 6 and Mass 28 in Eastham to the Cape Cod National Seashore–Fort Hill sign. Turn right onto Governor Prence Road. At Fort Hill Road, turn right again and drive the short distance to the sign for the parking lot on the left.

south side of this great rock to anchor a pulley for hauling loads of salt hay ashore. Rich in nutrients, the hay was used both as a garden mulch and as food and bedding for livestock.

Once you are atop Fort Hill, the vista stretching before you includes Nauset Marsh straight ahead with the Atlantic beyond and Orleans Cove to the right. Samuel de Champlain considered establishing a settlement here in 1605 but was thwarted by Native Americans and the unobligingly shallow Nauset Harbor.

Before you reach the Captain Edward Penniman House, a 150-year-old house will appear to the right. It was built by the Knowles family, who farmed land on both Fort and Skiff hills. The trail descends into a locust- and tree-filled hollow and swings around Captain Penniman's barn and house.

In 1888 Captain Penniman had his house built in the French Second Empire style. It boasted a lead-lined rainwater cistern in the attic and indoor plumbing! A prosperous whaleship captain, Penniman wanted his nineteenth-century Victorian home to be the most elegant in Eastham. History records Captain Penniman's displeasure at the equally elegant taxes on his grand house.

The Fort Hill Trail ends by passing through the whalebone archway across the road from the parking lot. Such gateways date back to prosperous Cape Cod whaling days. Although Nantucket and New Bedford are probably the best-known ports, whaling actually began on the Cape. The first commercial whalers were idle farmers who discovered the magnificent mammals washed up on beaches in late fall and winter. Shore whaling gradually led to deep-sea whaling, with cruises sometimes lasting four years.

16

Buttonbush Trail

How much do you really "see" while walking in the outdoors? Do you take time to stop and smell the flowers? Do you feel a tree's smooth or deeply furrowed bark? Are you in tune with forest sounds? A walk along the Buttonbush Trail will help you gain a stronger appreciation for the environment we so often take for granted. The trail was designed for the blind, but it can be enjoyed by all. You might try closing your eyes and opening *wide* your other senses while walking this .25-mile route.

A guide rope edges the narrow path. Two-inch plastic discs around the rope signal the presence of signposts, while pieces of tape remind you to step cautiously ahead. The signposts (in both braille and large print) encourage you to stop often, touch, listen, and smell.

Contrasting surfaces pass underfoot. Your feet will pound onto hard-packed sand, crunch over soft pieces of shredded red cedar, resound dully atop a raised boardwalk, and slap harshly against tough macadam. Log steps make walking easier in steeply pitched sections.

Be prepared for sudden temperature changes. The comfort of a shaded path is quickly forgotten as you walk out into the sun's blazing heat. Returning just as rapidly to the refreshing coolness of a covered trail helps you appreciate the sun's strength and the forest's protection.

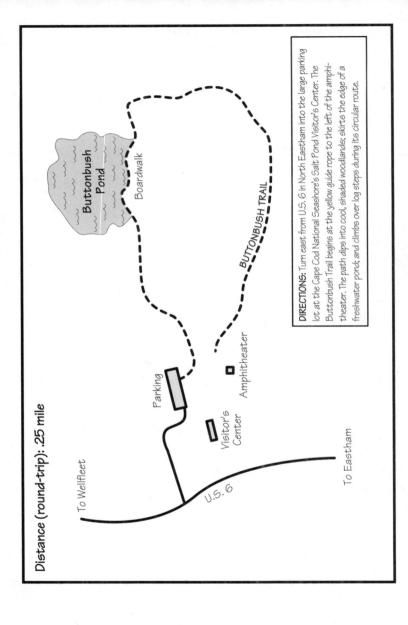

Distance (round-trip): .25 mile

To Wellfleet

Parking

To Eastham

U.S. 6

Visitor's Center

Amphitheater

Buttonbush Pond

Boardwalk

BUTTONBUSH TRAIL

DIRECTIONS: Turn east from U.S. 6 in North Eastham into the large parking lot at the Cape Cod National Seashore's Salt Pond Visitor's Center. The Buttonbush Trail begins at the yellow guide rope to the left of the amphitheater. The path dips into cool, shaded woodlands; skirts the edge of a freshwater pond; and climbs over log steps during its circular route.

Pitch pine, locust, red cedar, and other trees and shrubs await your touch and smell. Listen for the sounds of pond activity. You might hear the liquid call of a red-winged blackbird or the sudden plop as a frog leaps to deeper, protective water. While sitting motionless in warm shallows, frogs absorb the sun's heat and use it to accelerate their "cold-blooded" body functions.

The path nears Nauset Road. Did you really "hear" the automobiles? Listen for the clicking of chains and gears and the soft whirring of tires as the path swings right to parallel a bicycle trail.

Your final steps slap onto macadam as the trail slopes down toward the starting point.

17

Quashnet Corridor

The Quashnet Corridor follows the meandering and quiescent Quashnet River, a freshwater tributary that empties into the expansive Waquoit Bay on Cape Cod's southwestern shore.

The 400-acre property, parts of which were once slated for development, is now a state-owned conservation land and became that way largely through the efforts of the conservation group Trout Unlimited, which petitioned the state to purchase the $10 million acreage in 1988. The property is reserved for hikers, hunters, and fishermen, and the river is considered one of the state's best "catch and release" properties. The phrase means that fish caught there must be released; flies or lures are allowed, but no live bait or barbed hooks are permitted (fish will swallow live bait, and removing hooks will kill them).

The walk begins at a small parking area at Martin Road and follows a sandy, dirt road once used by commercial cranberry farmers. The bogs along the river have long been taken over by brush and semiforested wetlands, but the effects of cranberry farming are still evident. Along the main path, side trails lead to small cement dikes and dams that were once used to divert the river—therefore destroying habitats—for bog irrigation.

Today the river is flowing freely, and you'll see the occasional stack of wood or other construction material piled alongside the path. The material is used for the construction of overhead

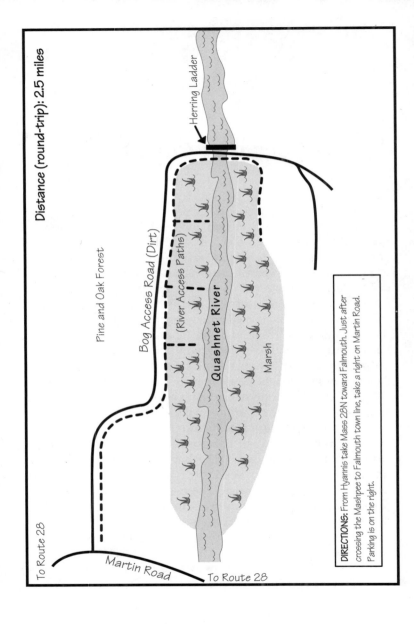

Distance (round-trip): 2.5 miles

Herring Ladder

Pine and Oak Forest

Bog Access Road (Dirt)

(River Access Paths)

Quashnet River

Marsh

To Route 28

Martin Road

To Route 28

DIRECTIONS: From Hyannis take Mass 28N toward Falmouth. Just after crossing the Mashpee to Falmouth town line, take a right on Martin Road. Parking is on the right.

covers and other in-stream devices that shelter trout as they make their way up the river.

The path passes through heavily forested scrub and white oak patches, with pitch pine continuing its relentless struggle to keep its hold in the woods. The thick undergrowth of low-lying bushes include sweet gale, bearberry, blueberry, and even the ground level wild cranberry. Small groups of poplar and black locust spring up, nonindigenous trees planted long ago to border the bogs. Swamp maple, black willow, and sassafras grow in the woods and closer to the water.

In summer catbirds, towhees, chickadees, the downy woodpecker, and thrushes are heard throughout the forest, and some of the smaller herons, including the black crown night heron and the green heron, have been seen in the woods. The usual mammal suspects abound, including white-tailed deer, rabbits, and the red squirrel; this last—a smaller version of its gray cousin—resembles an overgrown chipmunk.

The main road appears to fork in several places, but keep to the right, hugging the river. Take a few side paths down to the water. (They might be overgrown, and watch out for poison ivy.) At riverside, you'll be able to scan the clear water for fish. Among many other plants, reeds, cattails, and sparse wildflowers, including asters and steeplechase bush, grow on the banks.

After an hour or so, depending on your exploration time, the road forks hard right, where you'll find a small bridge. Underneath is a waterfall, actually a herring ladder. Herring migrate upriver in spring to spawn in its freshwater, and juvenile fish make the return journey to the ocean in fall.

Here you can climb down and walk along the riverbank for a few hundred feet. Gray birch, ferns, and, oddly, *Rosa rugosa* fill the riverside, and you may see a leopard frog on the banks.

The return path along this east side of the river is heavily overgrown in places, making passage difficult. Your best bet is to head back the way you came (about twenty-five minutes at a brisk pace).

18

Wellfleet Bay Wildlife Sanctuary

Wellfleet settlers reaped wealth from the sea through whaling and oystering until the blockade during the Revolutionary War ruined their economy. Desperate bartering with England and France restored the town's prosperity, but the Embargo Act of 1807 interrupted trade once again. Despite these economic disasters, Wellfleet's resourceful seamen not only persisted but prospered. By 1850 only Gloucester surpassed Wellfleet in mackerel and cod catches. The Wellfleet oyster beds were New England's richest. Today that era has passed, and tourism provides most of the income for the town. At the 700-acre Wellfleet Bay Wildlife Sanctuary, you have the opportunity to explore the area's natural history.

Information and trail guidebooks are available at the Nature Center (open daily from 8:30 A.M. to 5:00 P.M. in summer; closed Mondays from Columbus Day weekend to Memorial Day weekend. The trails are open year-round, daily, 8:00 A.M. to dusk, donations accepted). Walk left from the parking area to the sign for the Goose Pond Trail. Shortly after starting your walk, you'll pass Silver Spring Brook on the left. Silt and plant debris are gradually filling up the shallow pond formed by the brook's dam. Side paths poke through pond-edged greenery, allowing chances to glimpse pond life.

As you emerge from the pines, a vista across marshlands to the bay unfolds. Wild lupine abounds in the sandy soil edging

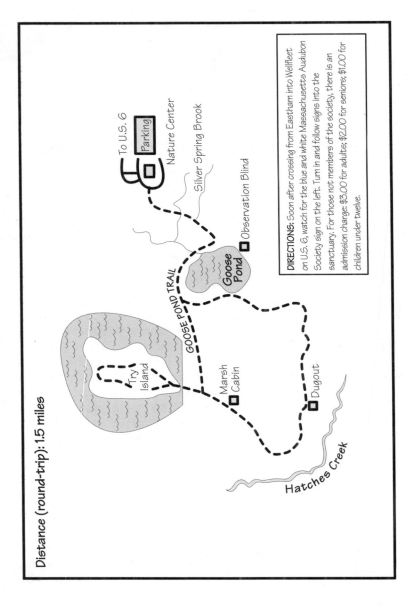

Distance (round-trip): 1.5 miles

To U.S. 6

Parking

Nature Center

Silver Spring Brook

Observation Blind

Goose Pond

GOOSE POND TRAIL

Try Island

Marsh Cabin

Dugout

Hatches Creek

DIRECTIONS: Soon after crossing from Eastham into Wellfleet on U.S. 6, watch for the blue and white Massachusetts Audubon Society sign on the left. Turn in and follow signs into the sanctuary. For those not members of the society, there is an admission charge: $3.00 for adults; $2.00 for seniors; $1.00 for children under twelve.

the trail. Note its pea-like blue flowers and radiating leaves consisting of seven to ten segments.

After approaching Goose Pond the path swings right. A small blind for observing and photographing wildlife is set on the pond's left shore.

The trail continues past Goose Pond, crossing a wooden boardwalk. Go right at the fork beyond the pond. As the main trail reaches a small cabin on the left, a secondary loop trail branches right to Try Island. Time a side trip to Try Island carefully or you may be stranded; at the time of the vernal and autumnal equinoxes, high tide inundates the entire marsh (with the exception of the island).

Continuing its loop around to the left, the main trail passes along the tide line and rises to higher ground. Tree swallows frequently nest in the birdhouses set atop poles along here. These birds are completely white underneath and are the only green-backed swallows commonly seen in the East. Their swooping aerial acrobatics and wide mouths aid them in capturing enormous quantities of insects. In cold weather they feed on bayberries.

Wintering eastern bluebirds and yellow-rumped warblers also eat bayberries, which are actually wax-covered nutlets. Candles are made from their waxy coating. When crushed or baked in the sun, the leaves give off a pungent aroma; bayberry's generic name, *Myrica,* comes from the Greek word for perfume.

The Goose Pond Trail finishes its loop at the fork just west of Goose Pond. Turn right onto this familiar part of the trail and follow it to the parking lot.

19

Atlantic White Cedar Swamp Trail

Both natural and historical features attract one to the Cape Cod National Seashore's Marconi Area.

Guglielmo Marconi built his wireless station on the crest of the high dunes rimming this section of the Great Beach. The station's first successful message, transmitted in Morse code, traveled to England on January 18, 1903, when President Theodore Roosevelt sent his "most cordial greetings and good wishes" to Edward VII at Cornwall, England.

Pounding breakers have reclaimed the sandy bluffs on which the station once stood. An excellent display and a three-dimensional model at the Marconi Station pavilion commemorate the people and places associated with the historic event.

Include, also, a visit to the nearby Observation Platform in your trip to the Marconi Area. Its 360-degree view takes in the head of Black Fish Creek, the narrowest point on Cape Cod.

A sign on the left side of the parking lot marks the beginning of the trail. The wood-chip-covered path winds through scrub oaks and pitch pine. Bearberry forms dense, evergreen carpets several yards across and a few inches high through here. In mid-May, note its waxy-white, urn-shaped flowers; pink coloring edges the flowers' small mouths. Dull red berries last into November.

Gnarled pitch pine archways deposit cushiony carpets of

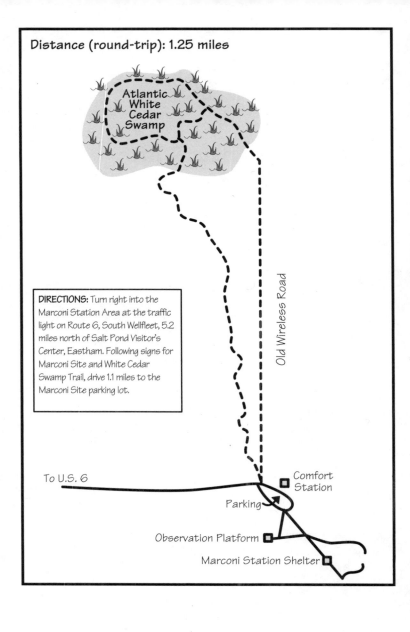

Distance (round-trip): 1.25 miles

Atlantic White Cedar Swamp

DIRECTIONS: Turn right into the Marconi Station Area at the traffic light on Route 6, South Wellfleet, 5.2 miles north of Salt Pond Visitor's Center, Eastham. Following signs for Marconi Site and White Cedar Swamp Trail, drive 1.1 miles to the Marconi Site parking lot.

Old Wireless Road

To U.S. 6

Comfort Station

Parking

Observation Platform

Marconi Station Shelter

needles on the path as the trail bends around an oddly misshapen tree. Log steps offer firm footing as you climb and descend among increasingly taller and thicker oak trees.

The trail swings left and leads through the Atlantic White Cedar Swamp via an elevated boardwalk. Stay left at the fork ahead; the right fork is an alternate—but much shorter—route through the swamp. This swamp began 10,000 to 12,000 years ago when glaciers retreated, leaving huge blocks of rock and soil-covered ice. When the ice blocks melted, the rocks and soil settled to form kettle holes.

Take time to enjoy the unusual swamp flora and (if you're lucky) fauna. Of course, the swamp's namesake is also its most imposing feature. Atlantic white cedar wood has been prized for centuries for its resistance to insects and disease. Indians fashioned canoes from its light, rot-resistant wood; American revolutionaries made gunpowder from white cedar charcoal. Cedar chests have preserved generations of clothing from moths and mildew.

Shortly after the alternate route enters from the right, you leave the boardwalk and the cool, humid cedar swamp behind. After climbing a short, gradual, sandy grade, swing right onto a wider trail. This is the Old Wireless Road, the original access route to Marconi's station.

Walk over the soft sand up this long, gradual incline to where you rejoin the wood-chip path. Turn left to the parking lot.

20

Great Island Trail

The arduous Great Island Trail requires sun hats, drinking water, sturdy hiking shoes, a fit body, and an early morning start to avoid the intense midday summer sun. (You'll also need to schedule the midpoint of your hiking time to coincide with low tide if you wish to explore Jeremy Point.) Yet the rewards are many, from glimpses of the feisty fiddler crab to the "natural high" that Jeremy Point's wind- and wave-swept wildness gives you.

The Great Island Trail begins to the left of the parking area and curls down between pitch pines to the mouth of the Herring River. Crunching salt hay underfoot, bear right at the water's edge. Early settlers fed their cattle nutrient-rich salt hay; current settlers still use the hay as a garden mulch.

Walking along the sandy road bordering the tidal flat, you'll see animal signs etched in the sand. Gulls leave alternating "walking" tracks, while sideways-moving fiddler crabs leave lacy tracings. These burrowing crabs dig subterranean communities up to 3 feet long in the drier parts of salt marshes and sandy beaches. Only the male sports the outsize, singular claw for which the animal is named. Though these claws are used primarily in mating-season battles, males seem to enjoy waving them threateningly at passing hikers.

Bear left at the base of the grass- and shrub-covered dunes ahead, still edging the tidal flat. Beyond the vehicle barricade

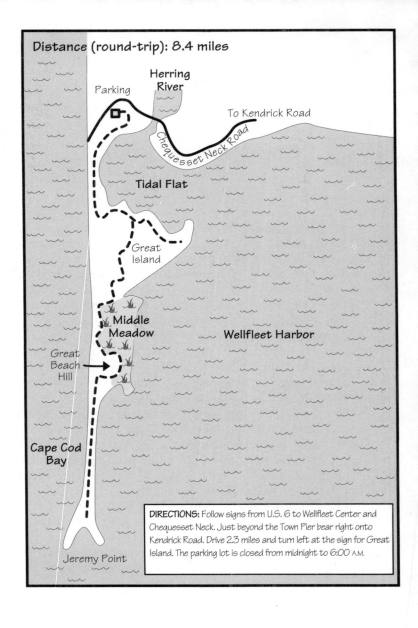

Distance (round-trip): 8.4 miles

Parking

Herring River

To Kendrick Road

Chequesset Neck Road

Tidal Flat

Great Island

Middle Meadow

Wellfleet Harbor

Great Beach Hill

Cape Cod Bay

Jeremy Point

DIRECTIONS: Follow signs from U.S. 6 to Wellfleet Center and Chequesset Neck. Just beyond the Town Pier bear right onto Kendrick Road. Drive 2.3 miles and turn left at the sign for Great Island. The parking lot is closed from midnight to 6:00 A.M.

ahead, bear right. (The path continuing straight leads to the old Smith's Tavern site.)

Marsh pea flourishes to the sides of the now narrower trail. Clusters of three to ten purplish flowers bloom from the ends of the long stalks. Each blossom's lower lip is lighter in color than the turned-back upper lip. The plant's paired leaflets are an appropriate pea-green shade.

As the grade increases, you enter a wooded area where pitch pines offer a welcome respite from blazing sun.

After you have walked 1.75 miles, a semicircular path leads left to a small memorial bearing a quote by Governor William Bradford of *Mayflower* fame. Rejoin the main trail and continue to the crest of a small rise for a view across grass-covered dunes to Cape Cod Bay. Descend to Middle Meadow, another low, marshy area. Once again you'll have to dodge the skittling fiddler crabs as they erupt from or disappear into their burrows.

After skirting the edge of the meadow, the trail bears right briefly, then swings left up over dunes. Look back from the top of this rise for a northerly view across Cape Cod Bay. On a clear day you can spot the Pilgrim Monument in Provincetown.

A sign at the fork ahead directs you left. Enjoy this cool walk through more pitch pines. Another expansive view of Cape Cod Bay appears just before you descend to a third marshy area.

The path makes a looping bend to the right before reaching a sign pointing to Jeremy Point. (If weary, head back now.) The 1.2-mile Jeremy Point trail begins atop low, grass-covered dunes. Quickly swing down onto the beach, take off your shoes, and enjoy a mile of solitary beachcombing as you follow this curling sand spit into the sea.

Return via the same route.

PILGRIM SPRING

Near here on November 16, 1620, the Pilgrims, on their initial, "Discoverie" trip up Cape Cod from Provincetown, found their first fresh water. The Pilgrims' chronicle, *Mourt's Relation* (1622), relates the tale:

"...*Iat vs downe and drunke our first New-England water with as much delight as euer we drunke drinke in all our liues.*"

Although location of the spring has been contested by some historians, ...ous borings from this spot have been checked and they match the ...ins ...nt.

21

Pilgrim Spring Trail

Although the Pilgrims selected Plymouth Harbor as their final stopping place in America, they initially dropped anchor in Provincetown Harbor in November 1620. While the women stayed aboard ship, Pilgrim men rowed ashore to explore and search for food and water. They discovered water at a spring in North Truro and spent their second night in the New World beside it. A quote from the Pilgrim's chronicle, "Mourt's Relation," helps us appreciate both our ancestors' writing style and their joy at tasting their first New England water: "Sat us downe and drunke our first New England water with as much delight as ever we drunke drinke in all our lives."

The needle-covered path leads through thick, pitch pine woods. Sandy in spots, the trail winds out into open areas and back beneath gnarled pines.

The path eventually emerges from the low, scrubby woods onto an overlook. You gaze out over Salt Meadow (a freshwater marsh) to sand dunes and the Atlantic Ocean beyond. Migratory waterfowl use Salt Meadow as a sheltered resting area during their semiannual excursions. In spring waterfowl parents lead armadas of young across the marsh's placid waters.

Great blue heron is one of the types of migratory waterfowl that may be observed in the Salt Meadow. This long-legged wading bird stands up to 38 inches high and has up to a 70-inch

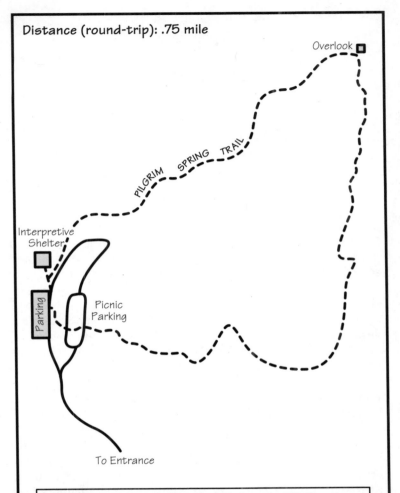

Distance (round-trip): .75 mile

Overlook

PILGRIM SPRING TRAIL

Interpretive Shelter

Parking

Picnic Parking

To Entrance

DIRECTIONS: To reach the trail's start, proceed 2.1 miles north on U.S. 6 from the junction of Route 6A and U.S. 6 in North Truro. Turn right at the sign for Pilgrim Heights area and follow the arrows to the parking area near the Interpretive Shelter. The trail begins between the end of the parking area and the shelter.

wingspread. In flight its neck and head fold back, wings flap surprisingly smoothly, and legs trail straight out behind. When hunting for small fish and frogs, the heron walks slowly through shallows or stands, poised with head hunched on shoulders before quickly thrusting its lethal bill underwater.

The trail descends a series of log-supported steps and narrows as it passes thick bramble patches. This area provides an ideal habitat for cottontail rabbits, although you will only seldom see these furry hoppers. If lucky, you might surprise one crouched in the middle of the path with ears up, nose twitching, and eyes wide with watchfulness before it bounds away.

The trail turns sharply right here and leads gradually uphill through thick forests. Leveling out, it leads through a picnic area and reaches the picnic area parking lot.

Continue straight across this parking area and follow the trail up to the parking area near the Interpretive Shelter.

22

Beech Forest Trail

Shaded paths bordered by lush greenery await you at the Beech Forest Trail in the Cape Cod National Seashore's Province Lands Area. Much of this gradual walk follows the edges of two freshwater ponds; the rest is a ramble through beech forests.

Thriving forests once blanketed this northernmost tip of Cape Cod. Unfortunately, however, early settlers from Europe showed little concern for preserving the natural resources. Clear-cutting, overgrazing, and forest fires obliterated the native forests and meadows. Shifting dunes and windblown sand threatened to destroy the Province Land settlements. In the 1800s strict conservation controls and beach grass plantings began to stabilize the dunes' movement.

The Beech Forest Trail leads right from the end of the parking area. The way swings left, passing clumps of the aptly named wrinkled rose with its heavily wrinkled leaves and hairy stems. Its blossoms are large and deep pink, but occasionally fade to white. On long voyages Colonial seamen ate the wrinkled rose hips to prevent scurvy. Today Cape Codders make rose hip jelly.

Trees and shrubs hug the path as you pass a pond and cross over a small wooden footbridge. In sight of the water, search for turtles, ducks, and wading birds. Watch more closely for the movements of water striders, dragonflies, and whirligig beetles.

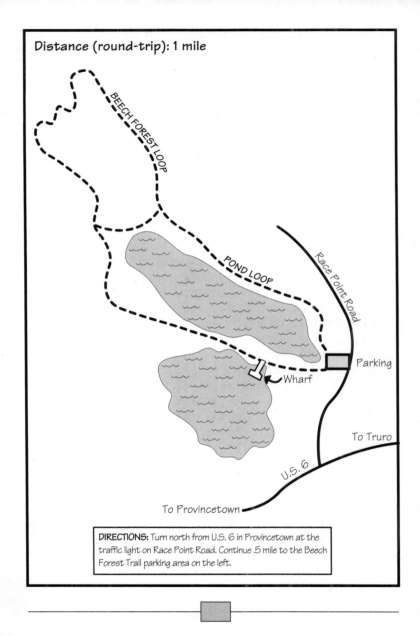

Distance (round-trip): 1 mile

BEECH FOREST LOOP

POND LOOP

Race Point Road

Parking

Wharf

To Truro

U.S. 6

To Provincetown

DIRECTIONS: Turn north from U.S. 6 in Provincetown at the traffic light on Race Point Road. Continue .5 mile to the Beech Forest Trail parking area on the left.

The footing along the main trail softens as the sand gets deeper.

Several different species of pine grow here. You can identify pitch pine by its bunches of three needles and its dead cones still on the branches. Scotch pine has rust-colored bark and bundles of two short, twisted needles, ½ to 3 inches long. Austrian pine has longer needles (up to 6 inches), which are also grouped in twos.

Oaks mix with the pine as the trail goes past rising sand hills and reaches a fork. The path to the left continues around the pond. Go right for a walk through the beech forest. These handsome trees have smooth, light gray bark and prominently toothed, elliptical leaves.

After about ¼ mile the way turns sharply left and climbs a sandy embankment. Logs cross the trail, creating a series of rustic steps.

The path labors downward over more steps and winds past dunes to the pond's other side. Shadows in the sand reflect the needled pitch pine branches above.

To the left, pond lilies almost smother the water's surface. Their thick yellow flowers become erect and bloom atop the large, protective leaves in late spring and early summer.

Ahead to the right a plank wharf protrudes into a smaller pond. Linger here in the sun and enjoy the isolated beauty. Wind and animal sounds keep you company.

Retrace your steps on the wharf and turn right to return to the parking area.

Nantucket

Regular flights between Hyannis and Nantucket, a twenty-minute hop, make getting to the island an easy jaunt. Regular flights are also scheduled between Nantucket and other airports in Massachusetts, as well as Connecticut, New York, and New Jersey. Two ferry services, the Hy-Line and the historic Nantucket Steamboat Authority, depart from Hyannis docks daily and will be able to transport you and your bicycle or car to the island. Advance reservations, particularly if you're transporting a vehicle, are required during the summer months.

23

Long Pond Trail

At the western end of the island, you'll find Madaket, a small village with a mix of contemporary and traditional Nantucket homes set on an expansive beach and harbor. Madaket is the site of the landing by Nantucket's first European settlers, a group of nine families. The village is bounded in the east by Long Pond, a thin and extended body of water—on a map it has the appearance of a flattened worm—created more than 17,000 years ago by receding glaciers. The pond is separated by a spit of sand from the Atlantic Ocean in the south and stretches northeast across more than half the island.

Long Pond is surrounded by marshlands, a bog, and low-lying grass- and shrublands that support a wide array of wildlife. Protected areas skirting the pond are managed by the Nantucket Conservation Foundation, the Nantucket Conservation Commission, and the Nantucket Land Bank Commission, all nonprofit organizations committed to the acquisition and preservation of local lands for scientific and recreational activities.

(Please note, for this and other excursions on Nantucket: Nantucket Conservation land border posts are marked by a distinctive logo, a gull flying above waves on a brown background; Nantucket Land Bank Commission land borders are marked by a post topped by green and white stripes.)

At the parking area a heavy wooden gate marks the begin-

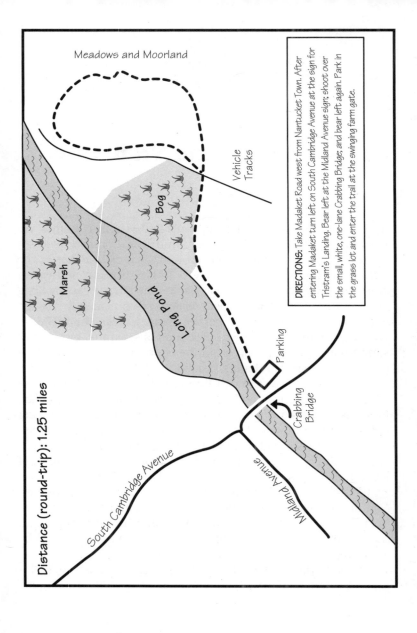

Distance (round-trip): 1.25 miles

Meadows and Moorland

Vehicle Tracks

Bog

Marsh

Long Pond

Parking

Crabbing Bridge

South Cambridge Avenue

Midland Avenue

DIRECTIONS: Take Madaket Road west from Nantucket Town. After entering Madaket turn left on South Cambridge Avenue at the sign for Tristram's Landing. Bear left at the Midland Avenue sign; shoot over the small, white, one-lane Crabbing Bridge; and bear left again. Park in the grass lot and enter the trail at the swinging farm gate.

ning of the walking trail. The walk here parallels the pond, and the homes of Madaket are visible over cattails, reeds, cordgrass, and marsh ferns across the quiescent water. On the upper-slope side of the path, you'll see shadbush and other shrubs, pink *Rosa rugosa*, mallows, heathers, and wild berry bushes. Beware of poison ivy; it's here and everywhere in woodsy sections of the island. At least one pair of swans frequents the area. Marsh hawks and the stick-like, 40-inch tall great blue heron are common, and osprey also visit the pond. Throughout the summer cottontail rabbits scurry about, and you'll probably see droppings, tracks, or other evidence of the white-tailed deer that inhabit the area. Rabbits and white-tailed deer are Nantucket's largest and most common land mammals. And while several mouse species and the field vole (a distant relation to the muskrat) can be found foraging in meadows, squirrels, chipmunks, and raccoons are virtually nonexistent.

Initially, the trail is angled, sloped on the pond's banks—a bit rough on the ankles but smooth and cleared otherwise. After a few minutes the trail bears east, away from the pond, to border a small bog, then follows a spoor cut by vehicles. A minute or two on the road brings you to a trail heading off to the right onto a vast plain of moorland and meadow bearing low-lying bushes such as broom crowberry, bayberry, huckleberry, bearberry, false heather, and scrub oak, as well as colorful clumps and fields of wildflowers. After about ¼ mile, the trail loop rejoins the vehicle road, where you can follow it back to the bog, pond, and parking area.

24

The Sanford Farm, Ram Pasture, and the Woods

It sounds like a mouthful, and it is—a walk through Sanford Farm and its richly diverse environs is one of the longer and more fascinating nature hikes on the island.

Sanford Farm and, in order from north to south, the Woods and Ram Pasture comprise 767 acres of small forest, wetlands, grasslands, and erstwhile farmland that today are preserved and maintained by the Nantucket Conservation Foundation. The lower woods and Ram Pasture, originally settled by local Wampanoag Indians, were called "the Long Woods" and "Nanahuma's Neck," the latter after a local sachem, or chief. The land was purchased in 1644 by Nantucket's farmers and made part of a larger, 29,000-acre "common lands," a cooperative holding used for grazing livestock. Surrounded on three sides by the fishhook-shaped Hummock Pond, the woods and pasture were naturally fenced in and provided ample water and pasture land for the animals.

The conservation foundation purchased the Woods and the Ram Pasture in 1971 and later, in 1985, acquired a northern parcel consisting of 133 acres of Sanford Farm, named after the former owner, Mrs. Anne W. Sanford. An additional 166-acre parcel of the original Sanford farm, lying to the west, is administered by the Nantucket Land Commission.

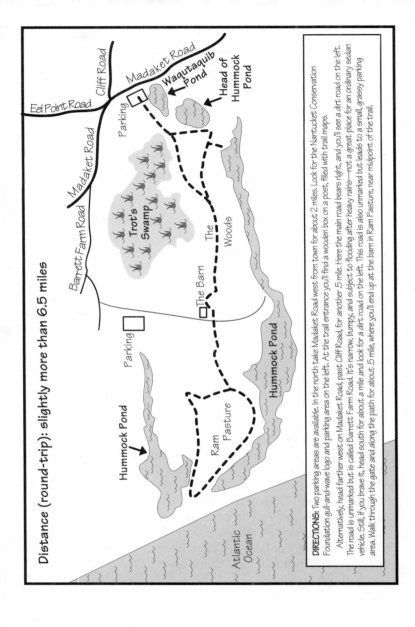

Distance (round-trip): slightly more than 6.5 miles

DIRECTIONS: Two parking areas are available. In the north take Madaket Road west from town for about 2 miles. Look for the Nantucket Conservation Foundation gull-and-wave logo and parking area on the left. At the trail entrance you'll find a wooden box on a post, filled with trail maps.

Alternatively, head farther west on Madaket Road, past Cliff Road, for another .5 mile. Here the main road bears right, and you'll see a dirt road on the left. The road is unmarked but is called Barrett Farm Road. It's narrow, bumpy, and subject to flooding after heavy rains—not a great place for an ordinary sedan vehicle. Still, if you brave it, head south for about a mile and look for a dirt road on the left. This road is also unmarked but leads to a small, grassy parking area. Walk through the gate and along the path for about .5 mile, where you'll end up at the barn in Ram Pasture, near midpoint of the trail.

The walking (or biking) trails throughout the farm, woods, and pasture total about 7 miles and in places are partitioned and looped, thus allowing walkers to traverse all or selected sections of the trails. More than twenty interpretive markers, some with mileage indicators, dot the trail and are cross-referenced on a map available at the head of the trail. The combination of interpretive stops and a fairly detailed map makes this not only an informative walk but also an easy one to follow.

At the Sanford Farms trail entrance, bear right up a small hillock. At 50 feet above sea level, this hill is one of the highest points on the property. Here you'll get an overview of the farm's land, with the large stone farmhouse of Anne W. Sanford, Waqutaquib Pond, and Head of Hummock Pond to the left and Trots Swamp to the right. On a clear day the ocean is visible 3 miles to the south.

Join the main trail—a wide swath of an old dirt farm road—and soon you'll pass a crumbled silo and house foundation, the remains of a dairy farm circa 1920. As the freshwater marsh Trots Swamp comes into view on the right, the trail forks. The smaller, left branch skirts the quiet Head of Hummock Pond and the marshy northern tip of Hummock Pond and soon joins the main trail. Head of Hummock Pond, a kettle pond formed during a glacial retreat 17,000 years ago, measures eighteen acres and 16 feet deep in places, making it one of Nantucket's deepest. The loop trail also passes through a small, fragrant pitch pine forest. The gnarled pitch pines, resembling overgrown bonsai arrangements, were introduced to Nantucket in 1847 by area settler Josiah Sturgis and thrive in the sandy, acidic soil and salt-dense air of seaside environs. The dominant undergrowth is the lowlying bearberry.

The right branch, the main trail, passes wildflower fields and moors of bearberry, huckleberry, bayberry, heather, and laurel, with Trots Swamp still visible on the right. Soon the trail enters the Woods and Ram Pasture through a set of wooden posts that once held a gate used to keep livestock in the common grazing area. The upper part of this vast area held sheep—in the eigh-

teenth and nineteenth centuries, mutton and wool were important commodities, so important that the annual sheep-shearing
time in June became an island-wide festival—while the lower
section, the Ram Pasture, held the rams, thereby allowing farmers to regulate contact.

At the lower end of the Woods, at interpretive marker 17,
you'll find a barn located on a small hill. The barn sits on the
border of a small parcel of private land, and from the hill you'll
have broad views of Hummock Pond to the east, as well as the
shore of the open Atlantic, from Cisco Beach to Madaket, to the
south and west. The path continues on to the Ram Pasture,
then forks to create another loop that, through prairie-like
grassland, skirts the eastern and western sections of Hummock
Pond. Hummock Pond was once connected at its lower end, but
the destructive Blizzard of '78 picked up huge sand piles from
the beaches to the south and dumped them across the pond's
shores, dividing it into two sections. Here you can step over a
fence for access to the beach.

Today the Sanford Farm's marshy areas are important feed-
ing grounds for waterfowl, including various species of duck,
geese, osprey, and terns. The meadowlands of the Woods and
the Ram Pasture support rabbits and deer, as well as short-
eared owl, ring-necked pheasant, and predatory hawks.

25

Windswept Cranberry Bog

More than 200 acres of woods, marshes, ponds, and, of course, cranberry bogs constitute Windswept Cranberry Bog, a functioning commercial bog and a Nantucket Conservation Foundation property.

The cranberry is a round, tart fruit of an evergreen shrub related to the heath family and belongs to the same genus as blueberries. The small fruit has long been big in the economy of New England and, particularly, of Cape Cod and the islands. Native American Wampanoags gathered the wild berries, which they called *sassamanesh*, and used them to make pemmican, a food that also utilized dried venison or beef and melted fat pounded and pressed into cakes. The Wampanoags used the cranberry in medicine as well, placing unripe berries on open wounds.

Soon European settlers began to use cranberries in food preparations, and whaling and trade ships carried the berries, rich in vitamin C, to prevent or cure scurvy among sailors. Commercial cranberry production began in earnest in the early nineteenth century.

Today cranberries are grown in bogs and sold through collectives to the large Ocean Spray company, located on the Massachusetts mainland. From June through early July, the bogs' cranberry bushes are covered by delicate pink flowers. Harvesting occurs mid-September through mid-November, a wonderful

time to watch the process in action. Bring a camera. In a process called "wet harvesting," the shallow bogs are artificially flooded, and paddle-equipped machines thrash and whip berries from submerged vines. The berries then float to the surface to create shimmering rose-colored lakes. The cranberries are gathered and shipped—Nantucket alone produces as much as 300,000 pounds per year and hosts what was once the world's largest cranberry bog, called Milestone Bog—where they are turned into jellies, relishes, and fruit drinks.

If you stop at a local farmer's market or grocery store in October, you'll be able to buy local berries brought in fresh, straight off the bogs. During the winter the bogs are again flooded, and a top layer of ice is allowed to form before water beneath is drained off. This layer of ice insulates the cranberry bushes from harmful frosts.

The trails of the hundred-year-old Windswept Cranberry Bog weave around a dozen bogs, passing through small woods, moors, and marshes along the way. And yes, it is windy.

At the entrance gate of the parking area, signs will remind you to stay out of the bogs themselves—your weight will crush the plants and berries. As well, bees are busy at work here, pollinating away and residing in beehives scattered around the property.

At the north section of the conservation area, the trails aren't marked but rather follow the general pattern of dikes and service roads that separate the bogs. Following these service roads provides access to the bogs and all their attendant wildlife, including the smaller bird species, such as finches, swallows, towhees, and sparrows. To the west a small trail passes a meadow and dips into a forest.

If you feel the need to set a goal, head south toward Stump Pond, a small, man-made reservoir created to provide water to the cranberry bogs. After parking, walk for about ten minutes past the two large bogs on the left. Follow the trail to the left at a pool house, which is located on private property. Bear right, or south, after the next bog. Here the trail skirts a marsh and passes over a dike at the quiet Stump Pond, where you'll likely

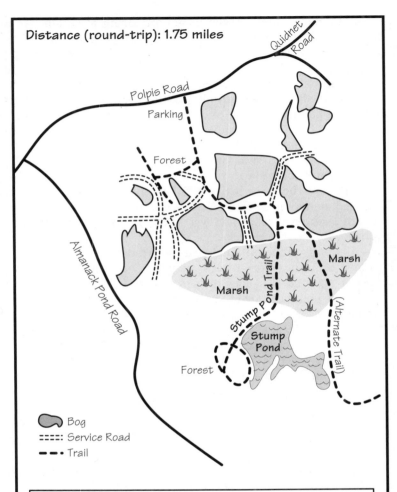

Distance (round-trip): 1.75 miles

Quidnet Road

Polpis Road

Parking

Forest

Almanack Pond Road

Stump Pond Trail

Marsh

Marsh

(Alternate Trail)

Stump Pond

Forest

Bog
Service Road
Trail

DIRECTIONS: From Nantucket Town take first Orange Street and then Milestone Road east; then take a left on Polpis Road. Just past Wauwinet Road on the left, you'll see a post on the right with the Nantucket Conservation gull-over-waves logo. Turn in for the parking area at Windswept Cranberry Bog.

see waterfowl such as ducks and heron. The trail then forks three ways. Right or left offers a loop around, and straight provides a path through another small forest of oak, maple, and sassafras trees. The walk is flat and easy, good for children, and punctuated occasionally by the loud hum of engines at water-pumping stations located around the property.

Martha's Vineyard

Ferries from Woods Hole, Falmouth Heights, and Hyannis will get you to Martha's Vineyard, but advance reservations are required if you are traveling during summer months with a car or bike.

26

Waskosim's Rock Reservation

The 167-acre Waskosim's Rock Reservation is splashed across the West Tisbury–Chilmark line in the bucolic Mill Brook Valley at the island's western end. The land was acquired, in an effort spearheaded by the Vineyard Conservation Society, by the Martha's Vineyard Land Bank Commission in a series of purchases from 1988 to 1994. This reservation is a richly diverse area of woodlands, meadows, and pastures; hills with panoramic views; the marshlands of Mill Brook; and no small amount of history.

The reservation supports several rare and endangered plant and animal species, and these were partially the reason for the conservation society's involvement in saving the land. The endangered cranefly orchid *(Tipularia discolor)* was virtually eliminated throughout New England by unfettered development. Martha's Vineyard is now the only New England location where it's found. The threatened American brook lamprey *(Lampetra appendix),* a filter-feeding fish sensitive to even low pollution levels, lives tenuously in the clean waters of Mill Brook. The eastern box turtle *(Terrapene carolina),* of which only twenty-six sightings have been reported in Massachusetts since the late 1970s, makes its home, now safely, on the reservation. Ditto for the rare LeConte's violet, the green wood orchid, the bushy rockrose, running clubmoss, poke milkweed, hooked crowfoot, and the southern lady fern.

A series of five color-coded trails weave and intersect throughout the property. All five cover a majority of the property's acreage,

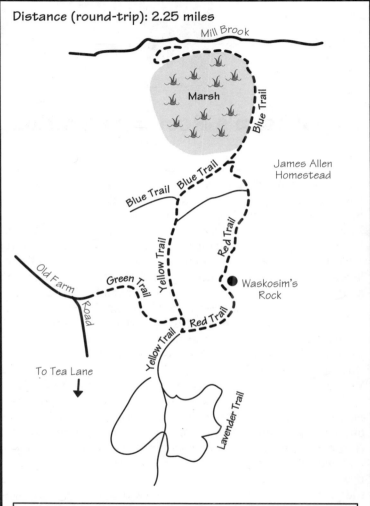

Distance (round-trip): 2.25 miles

Mill Brook

Marsh

Blue Trail

James Allen
Homestead

Blue Trail   Blue Trail

Red Trail

Yellow Trail

Old Farm

Green Trail

Road

Waskosim's
Rock

Red Trail

To Tea Lane

Yellow Trail

Red Trail

Lavender Trail

DIRECTIONS: From North Road in Chilmark, take Tea Lane, a dirt road, south for .9 mile. Take a left on Old Farm Road, and follow it for 1 mile to the trailhead.

but the Red Trail is a must as it passes the eponymous rock for which the reservation is named.

Enter the system via the Green Trail, which starts at the parking area off Old Farm Road. The trail passes a stone wall, goes through a white and scrub oak forest for a few hundred feet, and then tops a small hillock before it intersects with the Yellow Trail. Taking a left (north) will skirt Waskosim's Rock and point you toward forest and meadowland and the northern marshes of Mill Brook. Take a right and, after a minute, a left onto the Red Trail.

After a few minutes on the Red Trail, you'll see Waskosim's Rock, unmistakable because of its diagonal crack splitting the rock in two. The split gives the immense stone an eerie wide grin, and the rock was probably named for its resemblance to a breaching whale. The word, in the language of the Wampanoag Indians, means "whale turned to stone."

Waskosim's Rock is important for more than its imagery. The rock, deposited 15,000 years ago by a receding glacier, is a natural landmark. Although today it marks the boundary of Chilmark and West Tisbury, the land's first inhabitants considered it to be sacred. Ancient sachems, or chiefs, divided their land at the rock and used it for a reference point. In the mid-seventeenth century, the rock stood at the beginning of the "Middle Line," a stone wall running to Menemsha Pond in the south and separating Indian and settler lands.

Just past the rock the trail rises on a hill that, at 230 feet, is one of the island's highest points. The panorama of Mill Brook Valley lies below.

The trail continues north through meadowland for several hundred feet, past the seventeenth-century homestead of settler James Allen. It then forks left and right on the Blue Trail. Going right will bring you north through forest to deep marshland and Mill Brook, which features several ancient and sprawling beech trees. A short loop at the brook brings you back to the Blue Trail. Retrace your Blue Trail steps, pass on by the end of the Red Trail, and bear left at the Yellow Trail. Follow this trail back to the Green Trail, on your right, which leads to the parking area.

27

Cedar Tree Neck Sanctuary

Your outdoor tastebuds will enjoy a delectable, full-course experience at Cedar Tree Neck Sanctuary. The largest sanctuary under the stewardship of the Sheriff's Meadow Foundation, Cedar Tree Neck offers walks over varied terrain through woods, along ponds, and to the ocean. Birdlife and mushrooms abound.

There is no charge for enjoying Cedar Tree Neck Sanctuary, but donations are accepted and used for its upkeep as well as that of other Sheriff's Meadow Foundation properties. A large, mapped signpost near the parking lot shows the trail system and lists walking times. If you don't have the several hours this area (and you) deserves, base your explorations on the suggested times. (Swimming is not allowed, and the gate closes at 5:30 P.M.)

Follow the Red Trail's narrow, shady, meandering path. Red trail markers guide you over a small brook to a fork (both routes rejoin shortly). Low scrub growth and taller oak trees fill the trailsides.

Descend to the junction with the Yellow Trail and bear right across another brook. As your pace slows in deeper sand, you'll step into the open and see sand dunes with Vineyard Sound beyond. Cedar Tree Neck Pond is to the right.

Walking in deep sand becomes more laborious as you follow the Red Trail to its end at the beach. (Hurricane damage forced

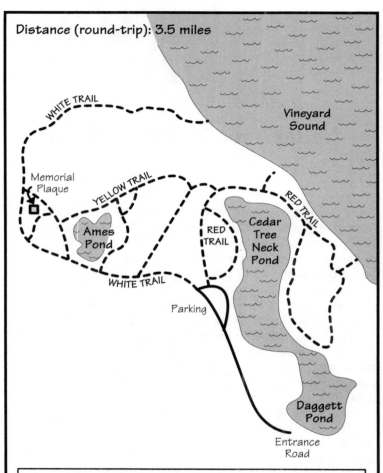

Distance (round-trip): 3.5 miles

WHITE TRAIL

Vineyard Sound

Memorial Plaque

YELLOW TRAIL

RED TRAIL

Ames Pond

RED TRAIL

Cedar Tree Neck Pond

WHITE TRAIL

Parking

Daggett Pond

Entrance Road

DIRECTIONS: From Vineyard Haven drive west on State Road. About 100 yards after Lambert's Cove Road joins from the right, turn right on Indian Hill Road. Follow Indian Hill Road to Christiantown Road. Follow Christiantown Road 1.8 miles to the sign for Cedar Tree Neck Sanctuary. Go 1 mile on the narrow gravel road to the sanctuary entrance. Take the short road to the parking area. (Remember: The gate closes at 5:30 P.M.)

the closing of the back dunes portion of the trail, which became a loop trail on the other side of Cedar Tree Neck Pond.)

If time permits, beachcomb awhile before returning to the junction with the Yellow Trail. Bear right across a gurgling brook and look for wildlife footprints in the mud.

Yellow trail markers lead you gradually uphill through smooth-barked, steel-gray beeches. Ferns, mosses, and mushrooms line the trail, and birds chirp in the woods. The trail bends around Ames Pond. This small, secluded haven contains several wood duck houses. Watch for these beautiful, crested birds and listen for their whistling flight.

At the junction with the White Trail, bear right and follow the short, steep path to a large hillside boulder. An inscribed plaque indicates the Alexander S. Reed Bird Refuge. Of the many birds observed here, one of the more unusual is the rufous-sided towhee. Watch for this fellow on the ground and in low bushes.

A variety of mushrooms dot the trail as it passes through taller trees before descending gradually to a damp, dark, spongy area. Cross the elevated catwalk and follow the sandy path to the shore. Views are more restricted here, but the crescent-shaped beach to the right invites walkers.

Return via the White Trail to the parking area.

28

Middle Road Sanctuary

Scattered clusters of rocks poking up through the earth atop a low knoll identify an Indian burial ground along the Middle Road Trail. The Wampanoag Indians on Martha's Vineyard had subjected themselves to the English king and God by 1675 and had become Christians. As such, they not only believed they were superior to shamans and invulnerable to their sorcery, but they also began to bury their dead, as the white man did. Some of these Christian Indians gouged symbols depicting various themes, hopes, and other statements on burial stones.

The extensive trail system through Middle Road Sanctuary (approximately 4 miles in all) offers an opportunity to "mix and match" short hikes with leisurely, lengthy walks. This pleasant walk on the Green Trail starts a couple of hundred feet west of the parking lot. It begins as a flat, grassy path surrounded by oak trees, which continue to proliferate along the trail.

The Red Trail joins from the left, and after gradual ups and downs, you reach a fork. Stay straight as the Red Trail branches left. When you begin to see the distant Atlantic Ocean through the trees, watch for the short, narrow path leading to the burial ground on the right. The Wampanoag Indians buried their dead in upright positions. The hiker is left to speculate about the placement of the stones in the burial ground. Do three stones

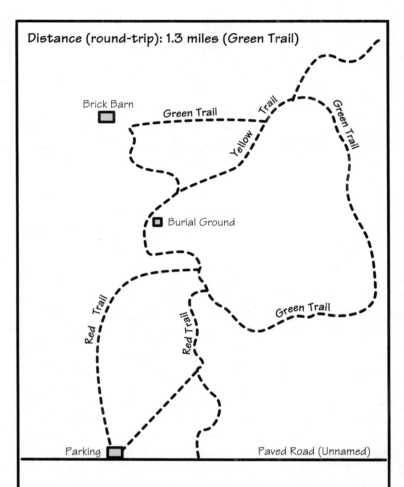

Distance (round-trip): 1.3 miles (Green Trail)

Brick Barn

Green Trail

Yellow Trail

Green Trail

Burial Ground

Green Trail

Red Trail

Red Trail

Parking

Paved Road (Unnamed)

DIRECTIONS: From Vineyard Haven follow signs for West Tisbury, Chilmark, and Gay Head 7.4 miles to the First Congregational Church in West Tisbury. Turn right onto Music Street beside the church. Drive .5 mile and turn left onto an unnamed paved road. Travel .5 mile and watch for the Middle Road Sanctuary sign on the left. Park on the side of the road.

side by side represent a family? Could a larger, more solitary stone mark the grave of a chief?

Return to the main trail. It descends Abel's Hill, crosses the Yellow Trail, and passes a large glacial boulder. Stone walls suddenly border the trail on the left and lead to a ninety-degree turn to the right. Stop here and look left to numerous stone walls and the only remaining brick barn on Martha's Vineyard. (Do not trespass on this private property.) Early settlers cleared stones from their fields and used the stones to make walls for boundary markers and to build pens for their livestock.

Stone walls and briers line the trail as it continues past an old sand pit and turns sharply right. Becoming sandier amid the ever-present oaks, the path descends gradually. A contemporary house brings you briefly back to civilization.

Following a sandy road, the trail passes more houses and intersects with the Yellow Trail again. You might go left onto the Yellow Trail to enjoy tremendous views across Chilmark Pond to the Atlantic Ocean. Just before a brick house on the left, the Green Trail turns sharply right and becomes a narrow path once again. The trail proceeds uphill, leaving the houses behind.

You may see wasps' nests hanging pendulously from trees along here. A female wasp makes the "paper" for her nest by chewing plant fibers or old wood. She then spreads the paper in thin layers to make cells where she will lay eggs. The nests found along this trail are constructed of many cells covered by paper with a single hole for an entrance/exit. This design is typical of two types of wasps: hornets and yellow jackets.

Topping a hill, the trail passes to the right of several more houses before eventually turning sharply right and returning to wooded seclusion again. Gradual, uphill meanderings return you to the original fork. Bear left and return to your car.

29

Manuel F. Correllus State Forest

If you like strolling beneath towering pines, standing quietly in the hushed silence and subdued hues of thick, closely bunched evergreens, and padding stealthily over trails layered with needles, put this hike on your *must* list. Pine-filled forests engulf you during most of this pleasant woods walk. (The forest also features 12 miles of bike trails and 10 miles of horse trails.)

Continue down the forest road for 100 yards and swing right onto the nature trail. The wide, grassy swath passes a sunken pond to the left and leads through rows of red pines. Unfortunately, red pines are dying out in this area due to a fungus infection. More hardy species are being planted to replace these pines.

Reaching a wide fork, continue straight ahead. Scrub oaks temporarily replace the pines to the left. Soon the thick rows of pines resume their domination of both sides of the trails. Eastern white pines begin to mingle with the reds as the comfortable path swings sharply left and back again to the right.

White pines have 3- to 5-inch needles in bundles of fives. Young trees have smooth, gray bark; older ones have dark, deep-furrowed bark. The largest conifer in the northeast, white pines once grew to heights of 200 feet and more. Due to extensive lumbering, especially for house construction, these trees today are seldom allowed to exceed 75 to 100 feet in height.

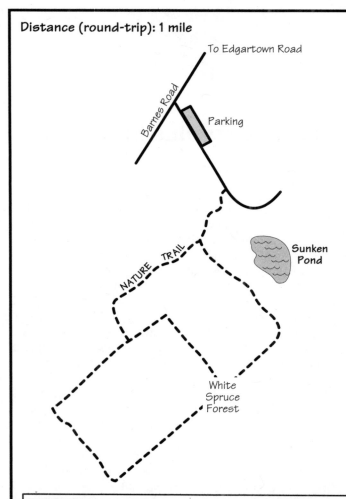

Distance (round-trip): 1 mile

To Edgartown Road

Barnes Road

Parking

NATURE TRAIL

Sunken Pond

White Spruce Forest

DIRECTIONS: From Vineyard Haven follow signs for West Tisbury, Chilmark, and Gay Head for .4 mile. Turn left at the sign for Edgartown. Drive 2.2 miles and turn right onto Barnes Road. After .9 mile turn left at the State Forest sign. The parking lot is immediately on your left.

After following a long straight path, the way turns sharply left onto a grassier trail. As the pines thin out, blueberry bushes edge the trail.

Turn left at the next intersection (following the nature trail sign). Ahead, pines litter the path with cones and needles; the needles are so thick that they feel like piles of hay underfoot. White pine cones are slender and 2 to 4 inches long; red pine cones are plumper and smaller.

Red squirrels may scold you from the protection of pine boughs. These industrious creatures are masters at gathering food. They will cut loose numerous nuts and cones in a single session, then gather them for deposit in underground hide-aways. They will also carry mushrooms up into trees and place them on limbs to dry.

The trail meanders through a white spruce forest. White spruces have four-sided, bluish green needles arranged in compact spirals around nonhairy twigs (red and black spruces have hairy twigs). Cones are 1 to 2½ inches long with thin, flexible scales. The tree's outer bark is an ash brown color.

The path swings left at the next intersection, and the sunken pond becomes visible through trees on your right. Turn right at the next intersection and return to the parking area.

30

Felix Neck Wildlife Sanctuary

Interpretive pamphlets guide you over miles of trails through open fields and woodlands and along marshes, beaches, and small ponds at the Felix Neck Wildlife Sanctuary. An observation hut enables you to watch and identify a living collection of native waterfowl. The nature center contains maps, booklets, exhibits, and a library with a good ecological and environmental reference collection. Knowledgeable staff and volunteers will answer your questions.

In 1963 George Moffett, owner of the land that now forms the bulk of the 350-acre property, and two close friends formed the Martha's Vineyard Natural History Society. In 1967 the land was donated to the Massachusetts Audubon Society.

Walk from the far end of the parking lot through the trees to the nature center (open 8:00 A.M. to 4:00 P.M. daily, June through September; closed Mondays during the rest of the year; trails are open daily sunrise until 7:00 P.M.). Browse through this building before beginning your walk. When ready to stretch your legs, go left to the Yellow Trail markers.

The flat, grassy path passes an open field and winds through a narrow wooded area, eventually reaching a small, semicircular pond. The blueberry-bush-lined Shad Trail exits left here. Follow it to the small, marshy strip at the edge of Major's Cove.

Return to the Yellow Trail and turn left through older, thicker

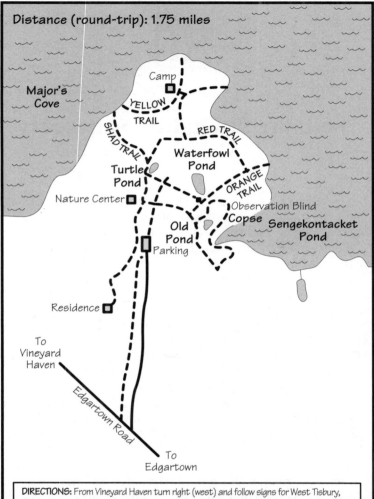

Distance (round-trip): 1.75 miles

Major's Cove

Camp

YELLOW TRAIL

SHAD TRAIL

RED TRAIL

Waterfowl Pond

Turtle Pond

Nature Center

ORANGE TRAIL

Observation Blind

Copse

Sengekontacket Pond

Old Pond

Parking

Residence

To Vineyard Haven

Edgartown Road

To Edgartown

DIRECTIONS: From Vineyard Haven turn right (west) and follow signs for West Tisbury, Chilmark, and Gay Head for .4 mile. Turn left at the sign for Edgartown and go 4.6 miles to the sanctuary entrance's sign (on left). Turn left and go .7 mile on the sandy access road to the parking lot. Nonmember admission fees are $3.00 for adults, $2.00 for seniors and children. Massachusetts Audubon Society members are admitted free.

woods. The alternately sandy and grassy path weaves in and out of wooded areas before arriving at a small, weathered building. The Yellow Trail passes by the cabin and slithers between high-bush blueberries. Poison ivy grows throughout this area and serves as a constant reminder to remain on the trails. At the end of the Yellow Trail, you can see the sandy finger of Edgartown Beach across Major's Cove.

Retrace your steps to the cabin and take the trail that exits left from the circular road in front of it. This flat path leads to a view of Sengekontacket Pond, where you can observe wild water-fowl and herons.

Return to the circular road, swing left, and follow it to the Red Trail. Turn left again. Fresh sea breezes will brush your face as you walk out to the shore of Sengekontacket Pond once more. Try whistling *bobwhite* to the quail that enliven this area.

Turn right onto the Orange Trail and walk to the observation blind at the edge of Waterfowl Pond. Here you can watch flocks of native dabbling and diving ducks. Because the sanctuary is located on a migratory flyway, numerous species of wild water-fowl visit the pond each year.

Continue on the Orange Trail back to the nature center.

31

Caroline Tuthill Preserve and Dark Woods

The 154-acre Caroline Tuthill Preserve and Dark Woods Trail (formerly called the John Tuttle Sanctuary Trail) was laid out in 1988. As the newest of the Sheriff's Meadow Foundation properties at that time, it represented another in the foundation's growing list of "forever wild" areas. By 1988 the foundation's properties were extensive enough to require the services of a full-time naturalist. The foundation grew, thanks to the dedicated efforts and leadership of founder Henry Beetle Hough and, later, his wife, Edith Blake.

This preserve offers a variety of natural features along its loop trail. The trail follows the gently rolling terrain, leading to both water and marsh views. Birders may have opportunities to view warblers and red-winged blackbirds.

The trail heads gradually uphill and swings left before passing a large depression on the right. It is all that remains of a barn built into the hillside many years ago. Just ahead bear left to begin the loop trail.

The trail winds through alternating stands of pines and oaks. Fallen pine needles carpet sections of the trail, cushioning footsteps and accentuating the quiet of the area.

The trail leads sharply left as you begin to see Sengekontacket Pond, then turns right and leads to a pond overlook.

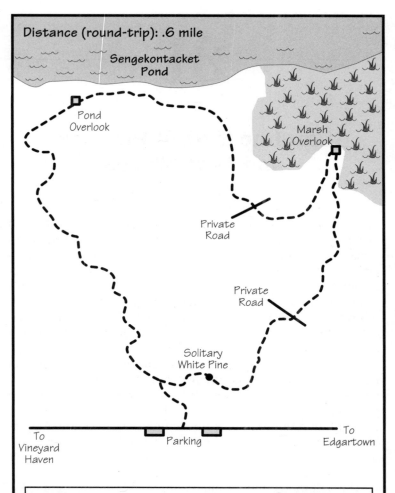

Distance (round-trip): .6 mile

Sengekontacket Pond

Pond Overlook

Marsh Overlook

Private Road

Private Road

Solitary White Pine

To Vineyard Haven

Parking

To Edgartown

DIRECTIONS: To reach the preserve in Edgartown (only one of the foundation's many sanctuaries on Martha's Vineyard), follow signs from Vineyard Haven to Edgartown. The entrance is on the north side of the Vineyard Haven–Edgartown Road, just before the triangular intersection leading into Edgartown.

Along the distant edge of this tidal pond, you'll see the Edgartown/Oak Bluffs Road. The pond attracts both migratory waterfowl and local islanders, who drag its water for scallops.

The path meanders away from the pond through an area with many clumps of reindeer lichen. This lichen grows in the soil in patches up to 10 inches in diameter. Its individual stalks resemble miniature deer antlers, and it is a basic food for reindeer in arctic areas.

After returning to the woods, the trail crosses a private road and switches back to parallel a salt marsh for a while. Both snowy and common egrets may be found within the marsh's confines. These birds frequent salt marshes and estuaries along the Atlantic seaboard. The common egret is the larger of the two, with a length of 32 inches and a wingspan of 55 inches. It has a yellow bill and glossy black feet and legs. The smaller snowy egret grows to 20 inches long and has a wingspan of 38 inches. Its bill and legs are black, but its feet are yellow.

Leading into woods again, the path crosses back over the private road, heads through oaks, and passes a solitary white pine. As the path connects with the original fork, bear left and return to your car.

32

Sheriff's Meadow Sanctuary

In 1956, from his home overlooking Sheriff's Meadow Pond, Henry Beetle Hough noticed that an icehouse had been torn down. Learning that the land around the pond was to be opened up for development, he bought the first parcel of what was to become the Sheriff's Meadow Wildlife Preserve, making his purchase with the $5,000 he had recently received for writing his first book. Borrowing additional money, Henry succeeded in buying all the parcels around Sheriff's Meadow Pond, but he couldn't afford to pay the taxes on them. He tried unsuccessfully to interest foundations in the properties and eventually created the Sheriff's Meadow Foundation himself. Over the years more tracts of land have been given to the foundation and new trails have been established. Donations can be sent to Sheriff's Meadow Foundation, Mary P. Wakeman Conservation Center, RFD 319X, Vineyard Haven, MA 02568.

The sanctuaries of the Sheriff's Meadow Foundation offer chances to escape from crowds and congestion, renew one's senses in natural settings, walk undisturbed, discover Martha's Vineyard's varied character, and see wildlife in natural habitats. Voluntary contributions support the foundation's efforts to preserve, administer, and maintain natural wildlife habitats for education and conservation. Hunting, trapping, camping, and picnicking are prohibited.

The narrow footpath weaves through pines and spruces be-

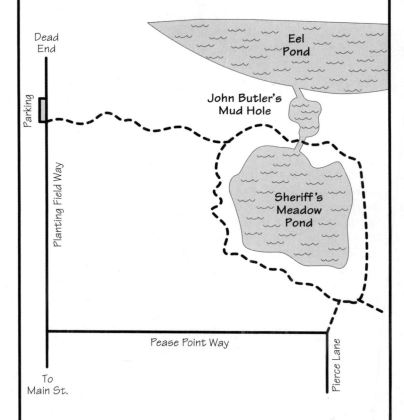

Distance (round-trip): 1.1 miles

Dead End

Parking

Planting Field Way

Eel Pond

John Butler's Mud Hole

Sheriff's Meadow Pond

Pease Point Way

Pierce Lane

To Main St.

DIRECTIONS: From Vineyard Haven follow signs to Edgartown. Turn left at the monument on Main Street onto Pease Point Way. As this road bends sharply right a short distance ahead, either continue straight .2 mile (on Planting Field Way) and park at the Shurtleff Pumping Station or follow Pease Point Way to its intersection with Pierce Lane and park there. (This trail description begins at the Shurtleff Pumping Station.)

fore leading into a meadow filled with oxeye daisies and young trees. As you reach a trail junction and turn left, you leave any reminders of civilization behind.

After winding through heavy side growth, the path suddenly opens out onto a watery setting. To the left is John Butler's Mud Hole, with Eel Pond and Vineyard Sound beyond. To the right is Sheriff's Meadow Pond, an old ice pond that now provides a haven for varied animal life.

Approach the wooden footbridge ahead quietly and look across Eel Pond for signs of waterfowl. One of the more interesting birds to spot is the common loon. Note the low silhouette; the large, dark head; and (in summer) the cross-banded back. Although the loon is silent in winter, its yodel-like laugh can be heard frequently during the rest of the year, especially at night. Powerful feet attached at the rear of the body give extra leverage in water but make for awkward movements on land. Loons come ashore only to breed and nest.

Cross the footbridge and swing right through a tunnel of trees. A clearing ahead momentarily breaks the closeness of overhead branches and provides another view of Eel Pond. Continue along the path as it tunnels through trees and shrubs. In this darkened setting use your ears to detect animal activity and your sense of smell to recognize flowering shrubs.

At another clearing ahead you can rest on a bench while surveying your surroundings. Listen for the red-winged blackbird's liquid *konk-ka-ree* call. The red, yellow-bordered shoulder patch identifies the otherwise black male. Females resemble larger sparrows, with heavier streaking and longer bills. The promiscuous males may mate with several females during each breeding season.

Continuing past the pond's far corner, the trail swings sharply right. Pitch pine needles soften your footing as you reach another clearing with views across the pond. The path winds through cedars and spruces back to the initial trail junction. Turn left for the short walk back to your starting point.

About the Authors

Whenever the Sadliers can escape from indoors, they are out of doors—hiking, walking, jogging, canoeing, camping. Their enthusiasm for nature is unbounded.

Heather attended Vassar College and received a B.A. in psychology and an M.Ed. in education from the University of New Hampshire. Hugh received a B.A. in sociology from Bates College and an M.Ed. in recreation from Springfield College. They have written three other books on hiking in Maine, Vermont, and Massachusetts. The Sadliers live on the Maine coast.

About the Editor

Karl Luntta is the author of *Jamaica Handbook, Caribbean Vacations, Virgin Islands Handbook* (all books published by Moon Publications), and other travel guides, and he has written and edited for such publications as *National Geographic Traveler, Caribbean Travel and Life,* the *Boston Globe, Modern Bride, Fodor's Travel Guides, Cape Cod Life,* and the *Cape Cod Times.*

Notes

Notes

Notes

Notes